GET SCRUM F.I.T.

FRACTALS, FOCUS, and FLOW for HIGH-PERFORMANCE

ANTHONY W. MONTGOMERY

Get Scrum F.I.T.: Fractals, Flow, and Focus for High-Performing Teams

ISBN: 979-8-9993425-0-8

First edition

Printed in the United States of America

For inquiries, contact: contact@getscrumfit.com

To my Lord and Savior, Jesus Christ, whose grace and redemption are freely given, though I deserve neither. You carried me through abandonment, rebellion, and countless mistakes, even sparing my life multiple times. I should not be here and take no credit. My survival was due to Your mercy and preordained purpose for my life. This book is dedicated to Your love that transforms even the most calloused hearts and broken lives. May it glorify You alone and, in Your ways, point others to the hope and salvation found only in You.

To my beloved wife, Jodi. Thank you for your unwavering love, endless support, and for walking beside me through every challenge. You have been a great blessing, showing me the true meaning of devotion. This book stands as a testament to the profound impact you've had on my heart and my life.

And to my children, Max and Mark. May you always know how deeply you are loved. This book is a reminder to always seek growth, embrace challenges, learn from failure, and live with humility, faith, kindness, and purpose.

"You can't change just one part of a system.
Every change affects the whole system."

—From *Thinking in Systems: A Primer* by Donella H. Meadows

CONTENTS

Author's Note

The ideas and practices explored in this book owe much to the foundational work of numerous scholars and practitioners. Elinor Ostrom's research on collective governance and Jeffrey Liker's insights into Lean principles laid the groundwork for understanding Dynamic Fractals and WIP Limits. Donella Meadows' systems thinking and her concept of leverage points provided essential guidance for identifying high-impact interventions to drive systemic change. Amy Edmondson's pioneering research on psychological safety and Teaming provided critical insights into fostering collaboration and trust within team environments. Richard Hackman's framework for team effectiveness shaped the emphasis on enabling structures, compelling direction, and supportive contexts in the Fractals in Teams (F.I.T.) Formula. Daniel Pink and Patrick Lencioni offered key perspectives on motivation and team dysfunctions. The work of Charles Duhigg and James Clear informed the integration of habit science into micro-commitments, while David Marquet's leadership principles inspired the use of Commitment Language. Additionally, the theories of Robert Putnam, Anita Woolley, and Peter Senge guided the concepts of social capital, collective intelligence, and systems thinking. Contributions from John Sweller on cognitive load theory, Donald Reinertsen on lean flow, and David Anderson on Kanban further refined these ideas. Lastly, the practical approaches of Craig Larman and Bas Vodde in scaling Agile practices were instrumental in shaping the system presented here. To all these authors, my deepest gratitude for their contributions, which made this work possible.

Since 2018, I have actively experimented with the F.I.T. Formula across mid-size to large-sized organizations, refining its principles through real-world application. Initially borne out of a need to coach large, stuck teams, the F.I.T. Formula was created and later applied to team sizes consistent with the Scrum Guide, proving its versatility and scalability. This iterative process, combined with the ideas above and my own research into the socio-psychological nature of Scrum, have shaped the F.I.T. Formula into a practical and adaptable system. The F.I.T. Formula is a product of continuous learning, grounded in both theory and practice, designed to address the dynamic challenges faced by modern Scrum teams.

The F.I.T. Formula works best when all its components—Dynamic Fractals, WIP Limits, Teaming, and Commitment Language—are applied as a unified system. Each element reinforces the others, creating a synergistic effect that drives sustainable transformation. Some may find this approach novel, particularly in its emphasis on leveraging structure and language, while others may consider aspects of it unconventional or even controversial compared to traditional Agile practices. It's important to recognize that results may vary depending on the team, organization, and context in which the formula is applied. As with any change initiative, the success of the F.I.T. Formula depends on open-mindedness, commitment, and a willingness to experiment with its principles.

My ambition is that this book inspires leaders to fashion environments where high-performing teams can thrive. By embracing the F.I.T. Formula, team-level social systems can be shaped to embody trust, safety, and encouragement, unlocking true potential, and driving meaningful, sustainable outcomes. Beyond immediate results, my aspiration is for these practices to embolden a long-lasting cultural shift—one in which organic accountability, collaboration, focus, and ownership become cornerstones of success. Whether navigating the complexities of team dynamics or revitalizing a stagnant team, I hope this book provides leaders with a practical approach and insights to transform challenges into opportunities for growth and excellence.

Introduction

The Fractals in Teams (F.I.T.) Formula

Welcome

Welcome to *Get Scrum F.I.T.: Fractals, Focus, and Flow for High-Performance*. This book is designed for Scrum Masters, Agile Coaches, Product Owners, developers, and organizational leaders who seek to elevate their teams from simply functioning to excelling.

If you've ever felt frustrated by inconsistent sprint results, team conflicts, or a lack of accountability in your Scrum practices, this book is for you. Through the F.I.T. Formula—Dynamic Fractals, WIP Limits, Teaming, and Commitment Language—you'll discover actionable strategies rooted in both theory and practice. Drawing from proven principles in Agile frameworks, behavioral science, and leadership, this approach addresses common team dysfunctions and empowers teams to achieve sustainable high performance.

This isn't a book of abstract concepts or idealized case studies. It's a practical guide built around the journey of the Swaggernauts, a fictional Scrum team navigating the challenges of delivering under pressure while transforming their dynamics and outcomes. Their story will inspire, teach, and equip you to bring these principles to life with your own team.

Whether you're leading a newly formed team, trying to reignite a stagnant one, or exploring ways to scale Agile across an organization, this book will provide the structure, tools, and insights to help you succeed. Let's transform the way your team works—together.

Scrum's Promise and the Reality of Practice

Scrum promises agility, collaboration, and continuous improvement. It offers a lightweight framework for tackling complex product development, enabling teams to deliver value in small, frequent increments. On paper, Scrum is brilliant. Its simplicity is part of its appeal. "Do a little, review it, and improve."

Yet, in practice, it's not that simple.

Many Scrum teams struggle to achieve the high performance the framework promises. Instead of thriving in fast, iterative cycles of delivery, they often plateau. Their velocity flatlines. Their retrospectives feel repetitive. Their sprints are marked by unfinished stories, unmet commitments, and growing frustration.

Why?

Because theory and practice aren't the same.

In theory, Scrum is an approach where self-managing teams organize around shared goals. In practice, human behavior gets in the way. People don't automatically collaborate. They disengage. They wait for others to act. They prioritize personal preferences over team effectiveness. These aren't issues with Scrum itself; they're issues with the social and cognitive reality of teams.

The result? Teams plateau. They produce just enough instead of their best. They fall into predictable patterns in which each sprint looks like the last, and improvement slows to a crawl.

But it doesn't have to be this way.

Why Teams Plateau: The Hidden Frictions Holding Teams Back

If you've seen a Scrum team struggle, you've seen at least one of these patterns:

- Low engagement: Team members show up, but they're not really "in it." They attend events, but they don't actively contribute.

- Poor collaboration: Silos form, and people retreat into their own work. Stories are handed off between roles instead of being owned together.
- Social loafing: When multiple people are responsible, no one must be responsible. Tasks remain in progress with no urgency. People wait for someone else to act.
- Low accountability: When people aren't held accountable for their work, commitments become suggestions. Sprint goals are unmet. Deadlines are missed.
- Lack of collective ownership: Responsibility for tasks is primarily individual and an "I" mentality is pervasive. There is no cognitive realization that the team wins together.
- Low empowerment: Team members don't feel trusted to make decisions, slowing progress and stifling innovation.
- Minimal cross-training: A lack of skill-sharing leaves the team vulnerable to bottlenecks when key members are unavailable.
- Low productivity: Effort is being spent, but outcomes remain minimal, and value isn't delivered efficiently.
- Low velocity and carryover: All of this adds up to slow delivery, with stories rolling over from sprint to sprint.

These aren't just random dysfunctions—they're deeply interconnected. Poor engagement enables poor collaboration. Poor accountability permits social loafing. Low velocity is often the symptom, but not the cause.

Most teams address these issues in isolation, hoping that better retrospectives, sharper goals, or stronger Scrum Master facilitation will fix it. But this approach fails.

It's because these challenges aren't isolated. They're systemically linked. Addressing one without addressing the others often causes a new problem to surface.

This book offers a new, holistic approach to address all the friction points.

Introducing the F.I.T. Formula for High-Performing Scrum Teams

The solution to these challenges is not one single change. It's a system of changes—a system that addresses the interconnected nature of these issues.

This book introduces a practical, proven method called Fractals in Teams (F.I.T.). The F.I.T. Formula consists of four key components that work together to tackle these issues holistically.

Here's the F.I.T. Formula

1. **Dynamic Fractals**: Instead of one large team, break it into dynamic, small teams of people. Three people is ideal; four is maximum. A fractal of two isn't a team; it's just a dyad. Therefore, go for three. Each fractal takes complete ownership of one story at a time. This fractal structure serves as a container for all the formula components.

2. **WIP Limits**: Limit the number of work-in-progress (WIP) items at the fractal and team levels. Instead of one story in progress per developer, each fractal works on only one story at a time. If the Scrum team has three fractals, the Scrum team WIP Limit is three stories.

3. **Teaming**: Use techniques like Mobbing, Swarming, and Pairing to speed up flow, resolve blockers, and promote cross-functional learning.

4. **Commitment Language**: Language influences our reality. Fractals use Commitment Language to make micro-commitments daily, creating transparent, psychological accountability loops that drive progress.

This approach doesn't just address surface-level issues. It addresses the root causes of disengagement, social loafing, and ultimately, low velocity. By structuring in Dynamic Fractals, enforcing WIP Limits, leveraging Teaming collaboration techniques, and employing Commitment Language, the system builds a new social structure for the team—one that replaces ambiguity with clarity, individual responsibility with collective ownership, and an "I" mentality with a "we" mentality.

Who This Book Is For

This book is for people who want to lead, coach, or inspire Scrum teams to perform at their peak. If you're reading this, you're likely one of the following:

- A Scrum Master who sees the team struggling with collaboration, accountability, or flow.
- An Agile Coach tasked with supporting multiple teams that are stuck in mediocrity.
- A Product Owner who sees story after story "in progress" with little movement to "Done."
- A developer or tester who feels frustrated by how slow, fragmented, and reactive the team feels.
- An organizational leader who wants to turn good teams into great teams.

If you've been in these roles, you've seen the problems. This book will help you solve them—not with theory, but with a practical, repeatable system.

How to Use This Book

This book is both a field guide and a guidebook. You can read it start-to-finish or jump to the part that addresses your biggest challenge.

Here's how you can use it:

- Apply it incrementally: If you don't want a complete transformation immediately, start small. Begin with Commitment Language. Experiment with a single fractal or two. Apply WIP Limits in the fractals or across the entire team on your next sprint. Then introduce Teaming in the form of Mobbing, Swarming, and Pairing.

- Apply it as a full system: For a full transformation, roll out all four components at once. Run a sprint with full Dynamic Fractals, WIP Limits, Teaming collaboration techniques, and micro-commitments based upon Commitment Language. This approach has the fastest impact, but it also requires a larger initial shift and carries more risk.

If you're a Scrum Master or Agile Coach, you'll find step-by-step guides for introducing each concept to your team and overcoming resistance.

Part 1: Understanding the Challenges

Before we dive deep into the formula, we need to talk more about the problem. What's holding your team back?

We'll explore nine common challenges that Scrum teams face, including:

- Poor engagement
- Poor collaboration
- Social loafing
- Low accountability
- Low collective ownership
- Low empowerment
- Low cross-training
- Low productivity
- Low velocity

Remember, these challenges aren't isolated. They're deeply interconnected. You can't solve one without addressing the others.

Why These Challenges Arise

If you want to solve a problem, you must understand why it happens.

We'll explore the psychology, social dynamics, and structural barriers that cause Scrum teams to plateau.

1. **Psychological Principles**
   - Low Intrinsic Motivation: People feel disengaged, lack a sense of purpose, and view their work as tasks to complete rather than opportunities to grow, leading to minimal effort and poor outcomes.
   - Lack of Psychological Safety: People remain silent, avoid taking risks, and withhold ideas out of fear of judgment or punishment, stifling innovation and open communication.
   - Excessive Cognitive Load: Juggling too many tasks in progress causes mental overload, reducing problem-solving capacity, decreasing focus, slowing decision-making, and increasing errors.

2. **Social Dynamics**
   - Weak Social Norms: If the team's social contract, or how they will work together, is weak, unproductive behaviors and habits take root. This lack of accountability erodes trust, fosters disengagement, and normalizes underperformance.
   - Lack of Accountability: People may avoid taking responsibility for their work, miss sprint goals, or fail to address challenges proactively. This leads to finger-pointing, unresolved issues, and a culture where commitments are seen as optional.
   - Social Loafing: When people believe someone else will step in, they put in less effort. The more people on a team, the more "wait and see" occurs.

3. **Structural Barriers**
   - Misaligned Goals: People pull in different directions, creating confusion, wasted effort, and a lack of focus on delivering shared outcomes. If individual goals conflict with team goals, people may prioritize their own objectives over collective outcomes, leading to delays or incomplete work.
   - Lack of Empowerment: If people can't make decisions or are micromanaged, they disengage, get frustrated, and become reliant on top-down direction that stifles initiative.

- Siloed Communication: If teams don't talk, people act in isolation. Critical information is not shared or delayed, causing misunderstandings, duplication of effort, and a breakdown in collaboration.
- Lack of Cross-Training: An absence of deliberate efforts to develop shared skills and redundancy leaves the team vulnerable to bottlenecks, over-reliance on specific individuals, and reduced resilience.

These issues aren't solved by another retrospective. They're solved by changing how the team works at its core. That's where this F.I.T. Formula comes in.

Are You Ready?

If you're tired of getting stuck on plateaus, if you're tired of "in progress" stories lingering for weeks, and if you're tired of relying on "strong individuals" instead of a strong system, this book is for you.

Let's transform your Scrum team—not with theory, not with fluff, but with a system that works.

Why the Formula Promotes True Transformational Change

What Is Transactional Change?

Transactional change is like a fresh coat of paint on an old house—it improves the appearance, but the underlying structure remains the same. The foundation is crumbling from decades of weathering. The electrical wiring is the fire marshal's worst nightmare. The plumbing is old, leaky, and potentially toxic. You see a problem, you apply a fix, and you hope it holds.

These changes are often reactive, short-term, and surface-level. Transactional change doesn't require people to change their mindset—it simply requires them to adjust their behavior in response to an event or a directive to achieve compliance.

Characteristics of Transactional Change

- Incremental: Small, localized adjustments rather than large-scale redesigns.
- Surface-level: It addresses symptoms, not root causes.
- Short-term: It provides immediate results, but the underlying issues remain.
- Prescriptive: Often directed by leadership or management as "fixes" to perceived issues.
- Compliance-focused: Team members comply with new rules but may not internalize or believe in them.

Examples of Transactional Change in Scrum Teams

- Checklists: Adding a checklist to a process. This minor adjustment creates surface-level, after-the-fact verification but does not address deeper collaboration or systemic issues.
- Switching tools: Moving from Trello to Jira addresses tooling, but it doesn't solve the underlying issues of poor prioritization or weak accountability.
- Enforcing deadlines: Managers tell teams, "This story must be done by Friday." This creates external pressure but doesn't teach the team how to improve communication or increase ownership.

While transactional change is sometimes necessary for quick, tactical improvements, it doesn't lead to lasting, systemic change. It doesn't shift how people think or how they work together. This is why Scrum teams that rely on transactional changes often revert to old habits once the pressure is removed.

What Is Transformational Change?

Transformational change is like completely remodeling the house—redesigning the foundation, layout, and underlying systems to better suit the needs of its occupants and to future-proof the home. It doesn't just patch cracks in the foundation—it builds a new foundation to prevent cracks from forming in the first place. It upgrades the dangerous electrical to avert fires. It replaces the outdated plumbing to avoid leaks and promote healthy living. Transformational change is deeper, systemic, and long-term. It requires people to change their thinking, beliefs, and behavior.

Characteristics of Transformational Change

- Systemic: It alters the entire system, not just parts of it.
- Root Cause-Focused: It addresses the underlying issues, not just symptoms.
- Mindset-Driven: It changes how people think, not just how they act.
- Sustainable: The change "sticks" because it's built into the team's social structure and workflow.
- Self-Reinforcing: Once established, transformational change sustains itself through social norms, peer accountability, and team ownership.

Examples of Transformational Change in Scrum Teams

- Moving from handoffs to co-ownership: Instead of developers handing off stories to QA, the team works together in fractals where they co-own the entire story from start to finish.
- Shifting from "I did my part" to "We finished together": Moving from individual contributions to collective outcomes changes the team's sense of accountability.
- Replacing status-based Daily Scrums with commitment-based Daily Scrums: Instead of reporting "I worked on story X yesterday, I'll continue to work on story X today, no blockers,"

people make small, daily commitments to each other that are clear, measurable, and visible. Instead, people might say, "Yesterday, I achieved my commitment by completing the initial coding for the database insert. Today, I commit to refactoring the code to improve readability and performance." This shift moves focus from past activity to future outcomes.

Transformational change takes longer to implement than transactional change, but the results are far more powerful and sustainable. Instead of treating symptoms, it addresses root causes. It changes the team's beliefs, language, and actions.

Key Differences Between Transactional and Transformational Change

Criteria	Transactional Change	Transformational Change
Focus	Behavior and compliance	Mindset, beliefs, and system redesign
Scope	Localized (affects one part of the system)	Systemic (affects the entire system)
Timeframe	Short-term, temporary impact	Long-term, sustained change
Initiation	Externally driven from management	Internally driven from team
Change Mechanism	Rules, mandates, and tools	Norms, systems, and social structures
Example	"Follow this checklist"	"Own the story together"
Impact on Team	Compliance-based ("I'm doing this because I have to")	Commitment-based ("We believe in this change")

Transactional change often "feels" faster, but it's fragile. It crumbles under pressure. Transformational change takes longer to embed but sustains itself over time.

How the F.I.T. Formula Promotes Transformational Change

The F.I.T. Formula is designed to be a transformational system—not a collection of quick fixes. It doesn't just patch issues like social loafing, disengagement, or low velocity. Instead, it addresses the deeper psychological, social, and operational root causes of these problems.

Here's how the four components of the formula drive transformational change:

1. **Dynamic Fractals (Small, Flexible Teams within a Team)**
   - Old Behavior: Individual team members focus only on "their work," leading to silos, lack of collaboration, and finger-pointing when things go wrong.
   - New Behavior: Fractals collectively own a story, fostering shared responsibility, social interaction, and collaboration. This approach eliminates silos and ensures the team works together toward a common goal.
   - Transformational Shift: The mindset shifts from "my work" to "our work." This cultivates collective responsibility, encourages cross-training, and enhances the team's ability to adapt and respond to challenges.

2. **WIP Limits (Limiting Work in Progress)**
   - Old Behavior: Teams have too many stories in progress, leading to multitasking, context-switching, and delays.
   - New Behavior: Each fractal works on only one story at a time.
   - Transformational Shift: Instead of juggling too many tasks in progress, teams focus on finishing. This shifts the focus from "activity" to "outcomes," promoting clarity, focus, and faster delivery. This also eliminates waste.

3. **Teaming (Mobbing, Swarming, and Pairing)**
   - Old Behavior: Blockers are met with silence and waiting. Team members say, "I'm blocked," and nothing happens.
   - New Behavior: The moment a person or fractal is blocked, mob the problem. People pitch in to unblock it together. Additionally, people swarm to move forward faster.
   - Transformational Shift: Collaboration changes from "ask for help later" to "solve it now." This reinforces urgency, trust, and responsiveness.

4. **Commitment Language (Micro-Commitments and Micro-Habits)**
   - Old Behavior: People use vague or weak language like "I'm still working on it," "I'll try to get it done," or "I hope to get it done today."

- New Behavior: Fractals make daily micro-commitments to each other. Example: "We commit to finishing the unit tests for story X by noon."
- Transformational Shift: Thinking shifts from "what can I start?" to "what can I finish?" The team moves from weak language to commitments. Micro-commitments drive momentum and accountability, creating a social contract between team members.

Why This Approach Works

Most teams (and organizations) fail at transformational change because they try to "train" their way to it. But transformation doesn't happen through training only—it happens through coaching and experience. People don't change their beliefs until they see new behaviors produce better outcomes.

The F.I.T. Formula works because it's experiential.

- Teams experience the structure of Dynamic Fractals when they see silos dissolve.
- Teams experience the focus of WIP Limits when they see stories get finished.
- Teams experience the collaboration of Teaming when they see stories move faster, and blockers get resolved in hours instead of days.
- Teams experience the accountability of Commitment Language when they see momentum build day after day and sprint after sprint.

Conclusion

If you want a quick fix, use transactional change. Add a checklist. Change a tool. Enforce a deadline.

If you want lasting improvement, pursue transformational change. Change the system. Change the attitudes. Change how people think, what they believe, and how they interact within a social system.

The F.I.T. Formula provides the tools, concepts, and structure for a complete transformation. It's not about tweaking what you have—it's about building something new. If you're ready for transformation, this book is your guide. Let's start the shift from transactional to transformational.

Turn the page. The F.I.T. Formula awaits.

Chapter 1

The Fractured Team: From Apathy to Action

The smell of burnt coffee and old microwave popcorn lingered in the air of the open-concept workspace at Agilion Technologies. It mixed with the faint hum of fluorescent lights and the relentless clicking of keyboards. Team Swaggernauts, a quirky nod to their self-proclaimed knack for APIs, sat in a loose semicircle, each of its nine engineers stationed at their desks, eyes half-glued to their screens, and the other half-glazed with apathy. The team was a diverse crew, each bringing their unique strengths and personalities. Tess, Nia, Sofia, Ethan, Liam, and Amina were the software engineers. Ravi, Mateo, and Harper were the QA engineers. Kira, as the Product Owner, brought the vision and often worked from home. To Alex Morgan, a freshly promoted Scrum Master, most of them were strangers, and building trust with this team was certainly uncharted territory.

Alex paused at the door of the team room, notebook in hand, surveying the battlefield. It wasn't a literal battlefield, of course, but it might as well have been. The whiteboard at the front of the room was an explosion of Post-it notes, scattered across columns labeled "To Do," "In Progress," and "Done." Most were in the middle column—a graveyard of half-finished stories.

Alex had hoped for a team with energy and ambition. This wasn't it.

"Alright, let's get started," Alex said, motioning her hands to signal the beginning of the Daily Scrum. No one looked up. Not immediately.

After a long pause, Tess, the most senior developer, sighed and pulled her headphones off, letting them hang around her neck. Her dark curly hair framed a face that looked like it had seen one too many bad meetings. Tess was sharp-tongued and fiercely independent. She had a reputation for questioning authority, which wasn't always a bad thing, but it made collaboration—the cornerstone of Agile—a struggle. To Tess, "teamwork" often felt like an excuse for endless discussion and wasted time. She'd worked in environments where independence ruled, and in her mind, she thrived when left to her own devices.

"Sure," Tess muttered, not hiding the sarcasm.

On the other side of the semicircle, Ravi, the QA Engineer, leaned back in his chair, arms folded. His chair squeaked as he tipped it just past its balance point, rocking it forward and back. It was the only movement he seemed willing to make. A perfectionist through and through, Ravi lived for clean code and airtight processes. He'd spent years fixing other people's mistakes, which had left him with a deeply ingrained skepticism of his teammates. Without a doubt, he trusted code more than people. His meticulous nature slowed things down, but his standards were undeniable.

"Let's go in order," Alex said, trying to sound composed. "We'll start with Tess. What did you do yesterday? What are you doing today? Any blockers?"

Tess shrugged. "Finished part of the checkout flow. Still working on the API integration. I'd be done by now if QA didn't keep flagging me for 'missing edge cases.'" She glanced at Ravi.

Ravi raised his hands, innocent as ever. "I don't write the edge cases, Tess. I just find them."

The tension between them was thicker than server-side latency. Alex braced for the inevitable back-and-forth but decided to intervene early.

"Alright, Tess, thanks for the update. Let's get clarity on which edge cases we missed in our refinement process. Ravi, we'll check in on your end in a moment."

"Whatever," Tess said, turning her chair back to her screen, headphones already halfway to her ears.

"No headphones," Alex said sharply. Tess froze mid-motion.

"We're not done," Alex continued, softer this time. "This is a team meeting, not a podcast. Please stay with us for the next ten minutes."

Tess's eyes locked on Alex for a beat too long. Then she dropped the headphones on her desk.

"Fine," she muttered.

Small wins count, Alex reminded herself.

Ravi's Turn

"Ravi," Alex prompted. "What did you do yesterday, what are you doing today, and what's blocking you?"

Ravi yawned, clearly unimpressed. "Yesterday, I started testing the login feature. Found issues."

"Found issues?" Tess scoffed. "What does that mean, Ravi? Be specific."

Ravi's eyes narrowed. "It means there are issues, Tess. Want me to paste the whole bug log into the ticket?"

"Maybe if you wrote better tickets, we wouldn't have to go on a treasure hunt every sprint," Tess fired back.

"Alright, stop," Alex said, louder this time. It wasn't a request. It was direct. Everyone stopped. Tess angled her head back, rolling her eyes. Ravi looked down, lips pressed into a thin line.

"We're not doing this today," Alex said, standing taller now. "This isn't about who's right or who's wrong. If we have blockers, we clear them. Ravi, after the Daily Scrum, you and

Tess will get together to work through the observations. Then, figure out exactly what's blocking you and plan to resolve it. Tess, I need you in problem-solving mode, not critique mode."

Tess folded her arms but didn't say a word.

"Okay?" Alex asked Ravi, looking directly at him.

"Okay," Ravi muttered.

The Other Engineers

Alex moved on, scanning the room. "Alright, let's keep going. Nia, what did you do yesterday, what are you working on today, and any blockers?"

Nia barely glanced up from her laptop. "Reviewed some code. Working on the billing module. No blockers," she said, her voice flat, almost mechanical.

"Anything specific you need support with?" Alex probed.

"Nope," Nia replied, her tone leaving no room for follow-up. Alex noted the lack of energy but decided to keep moving.

"Thanks, Nia. Ethan, your turn," Alex stated.

Ethan spun lazily in his chair, tapping a pencil against the desk. "I'm still on the admin dashboard. Fixed a bug yesterday. Today, I'll try to finish the analytics chart."

"Is 'try' the plan?" Alex asked, a slight edge in her voice.

Ethan blinked. "Yeah, I'll try to finish it. Hopefully I get it done today. If not, probably tomorrow."

"Okay," Alex said, unwilling to push further. "Let us know if anything comes up."

Next was Liam, who mumbled his update. "I worked on the CSS for the user profile page yesterday. I'm going to work on it again today. No blockers."

"Alright, let us know if that changes," Alex replied, marking down a note to check in with him later. The lack of collaboration was palpable.

By the time Alex finished going through the rest of the engineers—Mateo, Harper, Amina, and Sofia—the meeting room felt heavier. Each update came and went with minimal engagement, an obligatory exchange of words that barely scratched the surface of teamwork.

They were in the sixteenth minute now. "Kira, do you have any-thing for the team?" Alex asked, hoping to end on a more positive note.

The Product Owner's Pressure

Kira's face appeared on the conference screen. Her camera was on, but her attention was clearly divided. She sat at her kitchen counter, glancing off-screen every few seconds.

"Sorry, sorry," she said, tapping a pen on her notepad. "I'm... juggling a lot. I had two meetings with stakeholders yesterday, and they're pushing for updates on the new payment gateway."

She adjusted her glasses, eyes darting to her second screen. "They also want an earlier release date."

Silence.

Kira's assertiveness came from her years in sales, where every pitch felt like it could make or break her career. She thrived on high stakes and fast decisions, but her impatience often clashed with the team's slower, more methodical pace. She meant well, but her energy felt like pressure.

Alex knew what was coming next.

"What can be done to move up the timeline?" Kira asked, as casually as one might request extra cream in their coffee.

Tess barked a laugh that sounded more like a cough. Ravi leaned back in his chair, his eyes rolling so hard Alex was surprised they didn't get stuck.

"Nothing," Tess said flatly.

"Absolutely no way," Ravi added.

"Look, I know it's not what we want," Kira said, tapping her pen more rapidly. "But this came straight from the business. They promised a client we'd have it next week."

"We're mid sprint," Alex said, rubbing her temples. "You can't be serious."

"Dead serious," Kira replied. "And we're going to need an early demo before the sprint review."

Tess pushed away from her desk. "You know, it's wild how management gets to make commitments for the dev team without asking."

"They're not 'commitments,' Tess," Kira shot back, her voice tight. "They're business needs."

"Same thing," Tess muttered, arms crossed. "Commitments are only commitments if we set them."

Alex raised a hand. "Let's table this until after the Daily Scrum. Kira, you and I will talk after this call. We'll figure out how to set better boundaries."

Tess opened her mouth to respond, but this time she stayed quiet. Another small win.

Alex took a deep breath, scanning the room. "Alright, team, that's it for today's Daily Scrum."

No one responded. The shuffle of chairs and muted keyboard taps filled the silence as people drifted back into their own worlds. Alex stared at the notes in her hand, feeling the weight of the room's collective disengagement.

Post Stand-Up

After the Daily Scrum, Alex sat alone at her desk. Her mind raced. She needed more than just a plan. She needed a way to reimagine how this team worked—and fast.

A blinking cursor taunted them from the edge of her notes.

"Dynamic Fractals."

"WIP Limits."

"Teaming."

"Commitment Language."

These were the four components Eli, the Agile Coach, had previously hinted about. But how can all that help a team that can barely finish a sprint?

The sound of a chair scraping pulled Alex from her thoughts. Tess was walking toward Ravi's desk.

"Alright," Tess said, arms still crossed. "You win, QA. Let's see these bugs."

Ravi leaned forward, eyes still skeptical but less combative. "Yeah. Fine. But next time, write better API calls."

Alex watched them work, side-by-side at a single screen.

Small wins, Alex thought. Small wins count.

Chapter 1 Summary

Chapter 1 introduces Team Swaggernauts, a group of disengaged and dysfunctional team members at Agilion Technologies, struggling to function as a cohesive Scrum team. The chapter highlights their fragmented dynamics, blame culture, and lack of collaboration during a poorly managed Daily Scrum. The Scrum Master, Alex, is newly promoted and navigating these challenges. From Tess, the sarcastic senior developer who resists collaboration, to Ravi, the defensive QA engineer, and Kira, the overburdened Product Owner, the team displays a clear disconnect in their individual priorities and communication. External pressures, like unrealistic timelines imposed by upper management, add to the tension.

Key Developments

Alex begins addressing the chaos by introducing small but deliberate interventions:

1. **Taking Charge**: The team begins disjointedly. Tess and Ravi embody blame culture, Kira represents external pressure, and Alex stands in the middle, unsure how to lead, but taking charge to stop the infighting.
2. **Collaboration**: By encouraging Tess and Ravi to work together rather than argue, Alex subtly lays the groundwork for future collaboration.
3. **Psychological Safety**: Alex interrupts blame spirals and reinforces a problem-solving mindset, focusing on clearing blockers rather than assigning blame.

4. **Small Wins**: Alex recognizes that trust and collaboration are built incrementally, not overnight. The chapter ends with Tess and Ravi hesitantly working together, marking the first small step toward a cohesive team.

Conclusion

Chapter 1 sets the stage for transformation by introducing the challenges and the four key components for high-performance: Dynamic Fractals, WIP Limits, Teaming, and Commitment Language. These components will drive the team's evolution from fractured to functional. The recurring theme of small wins underlines Alex's realization that lasting change doesn't happen overnight—it happens through consistent, incremental progress.

Reflection Questions

- What behaviors in your team contribute to silos or low accountability, and how might you start addressing them?
- How do your personal interactions model the collaboration and trust you want to see in your team?

Chapter 2

Deadline Reckoning: Six Sprints to Transform

The CEO

Nathan was the youngest CEO in Agilion's history, a leader defined by the rare combination of analytical precision and a charismatic vision. His rise through the company had been unconventional—starting in product management, where he became known as a bridge-builder, seamlessly aligning engineering and business goals. When he took the helm, Agilion was mired in stagnation, held back by outdated processes and siloed teams. Determined to transform the company into a model of innovation, Nathan embraced bold risks and unconventional strategies.

"Talent is everywhere," he often reminded his team. "What matters is the structure we give it to thrive." It was this belief in systems over individual heroics that shaped his leadership. Though he wasn't a technical expert, Nathan had an uncanny ability to recognize potential in people—and knew exactly when to challenge them to rise above their comfort zones.

The All Hands

The lights dimmed in the main conference hall of Agilion Technologies, drawing the room into a focused hush. Conversations dissolved into murmurs, and then into silence as Nathan Cross, the company's

CEO, strode onto the stage. Tall and sharp-suited, Nathan exuded the kind of authority that didn't require raised voices or theatrics. His mere presence straightened postures and commanded attention.

"Ladies and gentlemen," Nathan began, his voice resonant and assured, "Today, we stop reacting. Today, we lead." The words landed with weight, their impact heightened by his deliberate delivery.

Behind him, the projector screen flashed to life, casting a bold title across the wall in crisp, modern lettering:

"PROJECT UXCELLENCE: THE FUTURE OF CUSTOMER EXPERIENCE."

The words hung in the air like a challenge no one had asked for.

Alex sat near the back, arms folded, heart thudding in her chest. The words "Project UXcellence" (pronounced *you-excellence*) sounded sleek, ambitious, and corporate—the kind of project that comes with tight deadlines, constant pivots, and impossible expectations.

Nathan continued. "UXcellence will be the centerpiece of our product line—a unified platform where customers can manage everything in one place: purchases, payments, subscriptions, and returns." He let the words sink in before delivering the punchline. "And it's going live in Q3."

Alex glanced at Kira, sitting one row ahead. Her eyes darted to the side like she was looking for an exit. Her face told the story Alex already knew: Q3 was only six sprints away.

The Challenge

Nathan pressed a button on a small clicker, and a slide of glossy mockups filled the screen—clean user interfaces, smiling stock photos, sleek payment flows. It was beautiful. It was also fiction. It didn't exist.

"We've secured stakeholder approval, executive buy-in, and client interest," Nathan said. "All we need now is execution." He clicked to the next slide.

Three bold words: "TEAM SWAGGERNAUTS LEADS."

Alex's heart plummeted like a stone, crashing into the pit of her stomach with a sickening thud. Her team. The team that struggles to finish a sprint without a ton of carryover stories or a blame battle. The team that argues constantly. The team that can't agree on anything.

"We chose Team Swaggernauts for this effort because I believe in them," Nathan said, pacing the stage like a general. "They've shown promise. Now, it's time to deliver."

Tess, sitting two seats from Alex, let out a low chuckle. It wasn't a happy sound.

"'They've shown promise,'" she muttered, shaking her head. "Guess he missed our last several sprint reviews."

The Aftermath

Fifteen minutes later, the all-hands meeting ended with polite applause. Nathan stepped offstage and was immediately surrounded by department heads, all of them eager to "align on next steps."

Alex lingered near the coffee machine, waiting for the crowd to thin out. The post-meeting buzz was always the same—people whispering to each other just out of range from the managers.

"Six sprints?" Ravi scoffed, walking up beside Alex. "To launch a platform like that? Hope Nathan's got a time machine."

"More like a magician," Alex muttered.

Ravi poured himself a cup of stale coffee, took a sip, and winced like he'd just swallowed acid. "And did you hear him say our team? Us? We can barely finish a sprint with two user stories complete, and now we're doing a full platform?"

Alex glanced at him, then back at Kira, who was pacing across the room, talking on her phone with an earpiece. She had that "calm on the outside, panic on the inside" look that every Product Owner eventually masters.

"Better brace yourself," Alex said. "We're next."

_____

The Confrontation

Twenty minutes later, Alex found herself sitting in Kira's cubicle, a small low-walled space next to the open work area. Kira sat at her desk, phone on mute, her head resting in her hands.

"Six sprints," she muttered, like she was still processing it. "Six. Sprints."

"Yeah," Alex said, still standing in the cubicle entry. "You okay?"

Kira exhaled slowly, lifting her head. "No. But I don't have time to not be okay. I'm already getting emails from three different VPs asking for 'status updates.'" She raised her hands in air quotes. "Status updates. On something that doesn't exist yet."

Alex stepped in and whispered. "Did you know he was going to name Team Swaggernauts?"

"Nope," Kira said, standing up and pacing. "First I heard of it was the same moment you did."

"Then say something," Alex replied. "Tell Nathan it's unrealistic. We need more time."

She stopped pacing, looking directly at Alex. "Really? You think he'll listen to me? Nathan doesn't hear 'No.' He hears 'Figure it out.'" She let out a bitter laugh. "And I'm pretty sure he just handed me the hammer and nails for my own coffin."

Alex opened her mouth to respond, but nothing came out. Kira's not wrong, she thought.

After a moment of silence, Kira leaned in, her eyes sharp. "Here's the deal, Alex. I'm not asking for help. I'm telling you we're doing this." She jabbed a finger on the desk. "Nathan already set the date. He sent it to the board. So, if we miss, it's not just our team that looks bad. It's me. My job. My reputation. If that happens, you think he's gonna remember it was 'unrealistic'?"

Alex felt her chest tighten. "So, what do you want me to do?"

"Lead." Kira's eyes didn't blink. Her voice didn't waver. "Get them aligned. Get them focused. Get them winning. Because right now, Alex, they don't believe in themselves. And if they don't believe, they'll never do it."

Kira grabbed her phone off the table, already scrolling through her email. "Start with something small," she said, not looking up. "But do it fast."

The Leadership Burden

The words echoed in Alex's head as she walked back to the team space. Start small. Do it fast. Easy to say. Hard to do.

Alex glanced at Team Swaggernauts from across the office. Tess was back at her desk, headphones on, staring at her code. Ravi was scanning bug logs, eyes squinting like he was searching for lost treasure. Both were doing their work, but not together. Not as a team.

And now, they were supposed to build a new UX platform—Project UXcellence—in just six sprints.

Start small, do it fast.

Alex approached her desk and noticed a sticky note clinging to the edge of the monitor. Someone had left it behind, and a quote, bold and deliberate, stared back at them.

"You can only elevate individual performance by elevating that of the entire system."
—Edward Deming

Alex didn't know how to lead a team to victory, but she did know this: She had to stop thinking about individual behavior "fixes" and start thinking about the system.

She jotted down the first small system change to make:

"No more multitasking during Daily Scrums. Everyone maintains focus."

If she could just get one thing to change, then maybe the next thing would be easier. Small wins count, Alex reminded herself.

"Hey, team," Alex called, loud enough to make Tess look up. She slid off her headphones slowly, one eyebrow raised. "Tomorrow's Daily Scrum. New standard. No more multitasking. Everyone pays attention."

Tess blinked. "You serious?"

Alex nodded. "Starting tomorrow."

Tess rolled her eyes but didn't argue. Small wins. They had six sprints. And this was day one.

Chapter 2 Summary

In Chapter 2, Team Swaggernauts faces an intense challenge as Nathan Cross, the CEO, publicly designates them as the lead team for Project UXcellence during an all-hands meeting. With an ambitious six-sprint timeline to deliver a revolutionary customer experience platform, the team's existing dysfunctions are thrown into sharp focus. Alex, the new Scrum Master, is tasked with the seemingly impossible: transforming a fractured team into a high-performing one under immense pressure.

Key Developments

1. **The CEO's Bold Announcement**
   Nathan's confident declaration sets a high bar for Team Swaggernauts, thrusting them into the spotlight and placing their capabilities under scrutiny. The announcement is both a challenge and an opportunity, forcing the team out of its comfort zone.

2. **The Product Owner's Frustration**
   As the Product Owner, Kira is caught between executive expectations and a struggling team. Her candid conversation

with Alex highlights the urgency of aligning the team, setting clear priorities, and delivering results.

3. **Alex's Turning Point**

   Alex identifies that systemic issues, not individual shortcomings, are at the root of the team's struggles. They resolve to focus on incremental progress, starting with addressing multitasking during Daily Scrums.

4. **The Theme of Small Wins**

   Alex adopts the philosophy of achieving small wins as a pathway to larger transformation. The first step is streamlining Daily Scrums to reduce distractions and foster focus.

Themes and Takeaways

- **The Weight of Leadership**: Alex's role as Scrum Master becomes pivotal in steering the team through high-pressure circumstances.
- **Systemic Over Individual Focus**: Recognizing that team dynamics, not individual faults, are the main challenge plants a seed in Alex.
- **The Power of Small Wins**: Incremental changes, like focusing during Daily Scrums, set the foundation for greater systemic improvements.
- **Navigating Executive Pressure**: Kira's frustrations emphasize the tension between leadership demands and team realities, a recurring theme throughout the chapter.

Conclusion

Chapter 2 underscores the enormity of the challenge ahead for Team Swaggernauts and sets the stage for their eventual transformation.

Alex's decision to focus on systemic changes and small, deliberate actions lays the groundwork for growth. This chapter highlights that even in high-stakes situations, transformation begins with one clear, intentional step.

Reflection Questions

- When faced with a tight deadline, how does your team respond?
- What is one clear, intentional step you could take to start your transformation?

Chapter 3

The Catalyst: Reimagining the System

The low hiss of the coffee machine filled the air as Alex leaned on the counter in the break room. The fresh brew dripped slowly into the glass pot below, one drop at a time, as if mocking them.

"Six sprints," Alex muttered under her breath, rubbing her eyes with both hands. "Six sprints to build a platform from scratch with a team that can't finish a sprint cleanly."

The thought hung there, heavy and oppressive. She stared at the dripping coffee, as if doing so would make it brew faster. Each drop resembled sand cascading through an hourglass, a reminder of how little time they had left. Time was running out.

"Staring at it won't make it go faster," came a familiar voice from behind.

Alex spun around to see Eli, the company's Agile Coach, leaning casually against the doorway. His gray hoodie hung loose over a plain t-shirt, and he held a half-empty cup of his own coffee—black, as usual. His eyes crinkled with quiet amusement. Eli often drifted in and out like a breeze through an open door—unannounced, unassuming, and true to form. He never sought notoriety and preferred that others receive the credit; he often appeared without warning, just when the team needed perspective the most.

"Didn't hear you come in," Alex said, turning back to the coffee pot.

"You're too busy fighting invisible battles in your head," Eli replied, stepping inside. He sipped his coffee, watching Alex like a coach sizing up a player. "You look like you're already planning your escape route."

"Not planning an escape," Alex replied, pouring a cup at last. "Just...processing."

"Processing," Eli repeated, nodding slowly like he'd heard that line a hundred times before. "That's what people say when they're trapped in their own heads."

A Team on the Edge

"They gave us UXcellence, Eli," Alex finally said, blowing on the sTeaming cup before taking a sip.

Eli raised his eyebrows. "They gave Swaggernauts Project UXcellence? Big swing for Nathan."

"Yeah, well, it feels less like a swing and more like a...push off a cliff," Alex muttered. "Six sprints, Eli. Six sprints to build a payment platform. That's not even the worst part."

"Let me guess," Eli said, tilting his head. "Team's not ready. Blame's already flying. Everyone's playing 'not my job.'" He grinned knowingly. "Seen it a hundred times."

Alex stared at him, stunned. "How do you do that?"

"Because I know teams," Eli said, taking another sip. "Yours isn't special, Alex. It's just stuck."

"I know we're stuck, Eli," Alex replied, frustration creeping into her tone. "What I don't know is how to get...un-stuck."

"That," Eli said, grinning wide, "is why I'm here."

Eli had spent years in the trenches of Agile transformations before becoming a sought-after coach. He wasn't the type to quote the Agile Manifesto verbatim or drone on about theory—he thrived in messy, real-world scenarios where teams were at their breaking points. Once a burned-out software engineer himself, Eli understood the exhaustion of endless stand-ups that solved nothing and retrospectives that recycled the same complaints. His career pivot into coaching began when he realized he had a knack for seeing the patterns others missed—the bottlenecks, the miscommunications, and the systemic dysfunctions. His trademark gray hoodie and casual demeanor masked an unrelenting focus on building systems that empowered teams. Eli didn't just coach; he challenged, provoked, and inspired.

The F.I.T. Formula: Structure Beats Chaos

Eli stepped up to the whiteboard on the far wall of the break room. He grabbed a marker, tapped it against the board twice, and started drawing: a large circle with four smaller circles inside.

"This," he said, tapping the big circle, "is your team."

He tapped the smaller circles one by one. "And these are the pieces of the system. Break the system, and you break the team. Fix the system, and the team fixes itself."

Alex leaned her head, confused. "This one of those Agile Coach metaphors?"

"More than a metaphor," Eli said. "It's the formula." He wrote four words on the board, each in capital letters:

- Dynamic Fractals
- WIP Limits
- Teaming
- Commitment Language

"These four components," Eli declared, his voice rising with excitement, "are how you turn a bunch of solo artists into a band."

Alex squinted at the board. "All of it sounds like a lot more process."

"It's not process," Eli quickly shot back. "It's structure. And structure beats chaos."

Dynamic Fractals: The Structure Lever

Eli tapped the first term, "Dynamic Fractals."

"Your team is not a team," he said bluntly. "It's a group of nine engineers working separately, doing their own thing," Eli said. "Too many siloed moving parts. People point fingers because there's no collective ownership. And if I get my tasks done by the end of the sprint, I'm good. It's not my problem. Am I right?"

Alex nodded slowly. "Yeah, Tess blames Ravi. Ravi blames Kira. Kira blames Nathan. Carry over stories occur regularly. If fact, we're lucky to deliver half our stories in a sprint. It's a mess."

"Of course," Eli said, stepping closer. "Big groups lose focus. Small teams win." He tapped Dynamic Fractals again.

"Your Scrum team becomes a team of teams," Eli said. "This is the structure lever of your system."

"Sounds like more meetings," Alex muttered.

"No, it's fewer meetings. Instead of coordinating with nine people, you check in with fractals. It simplifies everything," Eli replied. He stepped back and smiled. "Small, self-contained teams that still belong to the bigger team. Your Scrum team becomes a team of teams. In effect, we're 'scaling inward' with self-similar patterns to create underlying efficiency and order, like fractals in nature."

How It Works

- Break your large team into smaller, cross-functional sub-teams called fractals.
- Three people per fractal is ideal; four people, max.
- Fractal membership can change from sprint to sprint.

WIP Limits: The Focus Lever

Eli tapped the next line: "WIP Limits."

"Everyone loves to 'start stuff,'" he said, grinning. "Nobody likes to 'finish stuff.'"

Alex frowned. "We have nine engineers, and there are always at least nine stories in progress—usually more."

"Exactly," Eli replied. "And that's why you finish so few. You need to stop starting and start finishing."

He turned to the board and drew nine parallel lines across the entire sprint representing nine stories, each owned individually by a different engineer. "This is how you work now," he said, circling all nine. "But what if you only allowed one story at a time for each fractal?"

"You'd slow us down," Alex said.

"Wrong. You'd speed up delivery." Eli grinned.

"Less starting, more finishing," Eli said. "This is your focus lever."

How It Works

- Set a WIP Limit of one story at a time per fractal.
- Work only on that one story. No moving ahead. No side stories.
- Complete that one story before starting a new one. No exceptions.
- The fewer stories in progress, the faster they move to 'Done.'

Teaming: The Collaboration Lever

Next, Eli tapped the third phrase: "Teaming."

"This one's simple," Eli said. "You don't work alone. Ever."

Alex raised an eyebrow. "You mean Pairing?"

"Yes, but more than that," Eli replied. "This is your collaboration lever, even when you hit a wall. Mobbing, Swarming, Pairing—it's all about working together in real-time. And, when one struggles, you all struggle together."

Eli gestured toward Alex. "You've got a collaboration problem on your team right now, yeah?"

"Tess and Ravi," Alex admitted. "They argue every day."

"Then make them pair on a story together," Eli said. "Put them both on the same story and have them work together in real-time. No 'you do this, I do that.' They do it together."

"Mobbing, Swarming, Pairing," Alex said slowly, as if tasting the words for the first time.

"Mobbing, Swarming, Pairing," Eli confirmed. "Collaboration beats isolation. Every time."

How It Works

- Mobbing: The entire fractal focuses on a single task to clear a blocker.
- Swarming: The entire fractal focuses on a single story to deliver it faster.
- Pairing: Two team members focus together on the same story or task.

Commitment Language: The Accountability Lever

Finally, Eli circled the last phrase: "Commitment Language."

"This," he said, leaning in, "is your accountability lever."

"How?" Alex asked.

"Every Daily Scrum, you say exactly what you'll do today. Not 'working on it.' Not 'maybe.' A clear, actionable commitment," Eli explained. "Social accountability kicks in when you say it out loud to your peers," Eli said, eyes locked on Alex now.

"That's going to make people uncomfortable," Alex said.

Eli grinned. "Yes. Discomfort drives growth. But here's the thing—leaders go first."

How It Works

- In the Daily Scrum, each team member makes a specific, measurable commitment.

- People choose their commitment. No one imposes. This is key for buy-in.
- Example: "I'll complete the regression tests for story #144 by noon."
- Watch out for weak or vague language. No "I might" or "I hope."
- Everyone's commitment is reviewed in the next Daily Scrum.

Where to Begin

Alex stared at the whiteboard, the four bold terms standing out like guideposts.

- Dynamic Fractals
- WIP Limits
- Teaming
- Commitment Language

"Start with one lever," Eli said, wiping the board clean. "Small wins. If you want them to change, show them it works. Make it experiential."

"Which one would you start with?" Alex asked.

"Commitment Language," Eli said, tossing the marker aside. "Because if people can't keep their word, none of the rest will matter."

Alex stared at the whiteboard, the words hanging in the air like a challenge. Commitment Language sounded simple, almost deceptively so. But something about Eli's tone made it clear: This wasn't just another tool or technique. It was a shift—a way to demand more clarity, more accountability, and more trust from a team that had none.

"I'll start with it," Alex said finally, her voice firm. "But how do I get the team to buy in?"

Eli smiled, stepping back toward the door. "The same way you'll want them to handle their work: one step at a time. Build the habit, and the trust will follow."

One More Thing

Eli grabbed his coffee cup and turned back to Alex, his expression thoughtful. "Oh, one more thing," he said, leaning against the counter. "For the next six sprints, keep the fractals fixed. No rotations, no changes."

Alex raised an eyebrow. "But isn't the idea to let the team self-organize? To adapt?"

"Eventually, yes," Eli said, nodding. "That's the 'Ha' and 'Ri' stages of growth—adapting and mastering. But right now, your team is in 'Shu.' You know what that means?"

Alex hesitated. "The basics? Following the rules? Be prescriptive?"

"Exactly," Eli said. "Right now, they don't need flexibility. They need stability. They need guidance. The dysfunctions in your team— finger-pointing, lack of trust, silos—won't disappear overnight. And with six sprints to deliver, you don't have a lot of time to experiment with rotations or self-selection. You need people working together, building trust, and focusing on finishing work. Fixed fractals give them a safe structure to do that."

Alex folded her arms, processing. "So, it's about minimizing distractions?"

"Distractions and resistance," Eli confirmed. "If you start moving people around too soon, they'll spend more time figuring out how to work together than actually working. Give them at least three sprints of stability. Let them experience what success feels like as a unit. Once they see it works, then you can introduce flexibility. For now, keep it simple and focused. Master the fundamentals first."

Alex nodded slowly, the gears turning. "Shu, then Ha, then Ri."

Eli grinned. "Exactly. Build the foundation, Alex. The rest will follow."

Alex glanced at the whiteboard one last time before heading to the team room, her mind racing with what the next day's Daily Scrum might look like.

Chapter 3 Summary

In Chapter 3, Eli, the Agile Coach, steps in as a mentor to guide Alex through the overwhelming challenge of transforming Team Swaggernauts. With the pressure of delivering Project UXcellence in six sprints, Eli introduces the F.I.T. Formula as a structured, actionable framework for turning a struggling team into a high-performing one.

Key Developments

1. **The Mentor's Arrival**
   - Eli enters as a calm and experienced mentor, offering Alex clarity and reassurance in the face of mounting pressure.
2. **Alex's Turning Point**
   - Alex fully embraces the idea of systemic transformation as the key to unlocking the team's potential.
3. **Focus on Small Wins**
   - Eli advises focusing on small, incremental changes, starting with Commitment Language, to build momentum and confidence. A **Shu stance** is recommended, favoring stability over flexibility due to the team's current dysfunction and tight deadline.

Key Concepts

1. **Dynamic Fractals for Ownership and Responsibility**
   - Smaller, cross-functional sub-teams of three to four members provide structure and assign clear responsibilities, fostering collective ownership of stories.
   - By reducing silos, eliminating finger-pointing, and sharing successes and failures, fractals promote a culture of responsibility and collaboration.

2. **WIP Limits for Focus and Flow**
   - Restricting work in progress helps fractals prioritize finishing over starting, enabling a steady flow of work while reducing context-switching and improving delivery speed.
   - This approach prevents the "start everything, finish nothing" trap while lowering cognitive load and ensuring higher-quality outcomes.

3. **Teaming for Collaboration and Cohesion**
   - Techniques like Mobbing, Swarming, and Pairing encourage real-time problem-solving, strengthen team cohesion, and improve knowledge-sharing across disciplines.

4. **Commitment Language for Accountability**
   - Team members make specific, measurable commitments during daily standups, fostering accountability by tying progress to explicit outcomes.
   - This practice ensures team alignment, builds trust, and reinforces follow-through by publicly reviewing commitments daily.

5. **Shu Stance for Structured Growth**
   - A prescriptive, structured approach during early stages of transformation helps teams focus, minimizes distractions, and builds foundational habits that support long-term maturity.

Themes and Takeaways

1. **The Role of Mentorship**
   - Eli's guidance highlights the importance of mentorship in navigating challenges, providing clarity, confidence, and support during transformations.

2. **Systemic Change Over Quick Fixes**
   - Sustainable improvement requires addressing systemic challenges rather than relying on temporary fixes or focusing solely on individuals, ensuring long-term team success.
3. **Building Momentum Through Small Wins**
   - Achieving incremental successes builds trust, boosts morale, and creates a foundation for sustained team growth and transformation.

Conclusion

Chapter 3 marks the beginning of Alex's transformation as a leader, guided by Eli and the introduction of the F.I.T. Formula. By focusing on systemic change and incremental progress, Alex gains a clearer vision for leading Team Swaggernauts toward success, setting the stage for their journey of growth and accountability.

Reflection Questions

- How does your current environment or systems encourage or hinder collaboration and ownership?
- What small, intentional adjustments could you make to improve collaboration and engagement?

Chapter 4

The First Commitment: Small Promises, Big Wins

A New Day

On the first morning of Sprint One—charged with delivering fifteen critical features for Project UXcellence—Alex arrived at the team room ten minutes early, coffee in hand and Eli's advice from the day before still fresh in mind. Commitment Language—it was about accountability, specificity, and transparency. It sounded good in theory, but now Alex had to bring it to life in front of a team that had long since stopped trusting each other, let alone their new Scrum Master.

Tess and Ravi were already in the room, each buried in their laptops. Neither looked up when Alex walked in. The tension between them felt unmistakable, a reminder of just how much work lay ahead.

"Morning," Alex said, setting her cup on the table. She opened her notebook and began sketching out the Daily Scrum questions she'd rehearsed a dozen times the night before. The first step to change, Eli had said, was to make it experiential. So today, Alex was going to make the Daily Scrum about commitments—real, clear, actionable commitments.

A New Daily Scrum

"Here's what's about to happen," Alex said, standing at the front of the semi-circle of desks. Her eyes moved from face to face, taking in the reactions of each team member. Tess, arms crossed, leaned back in her chair like a courtroom defendant waiting for a weak argument to fall apart. Ravi, slouched in his chair, tapped a pen against his notepad, the click-click-click counting the seconds. Kira was on video call, face framed in a box on the large conference screen, her brows raised in mild suspicion. The other team members stared at Alex in anticipation.

Alex felt the weight of it all. It wasn't just a team meeting. This was the line in the sand.

"Starting today," Alex continued, "we're changing how we do the Daily Scrum."

Ravi groaned audibly. "Oh, come on."

"Hold on," Alex said, raising a hand. "This isn't just some random new gimmick. It's simple, but powerful. From now on, when we give our updates, we don't just say 'I'm working on it.' We make commitments. Real ones."

Tess raised a hand, but not like she had a question. More like she was about to call a foul. "Define 'real commitments,' Alex. I don't like where this is going."

Alex stepped forward, keeping her eyes on Tess. "Real commitments mean no fluff. No 'I'm working on it,' no 'I'm looking into it.' Instead, you say exactly what you'll complete by the end of the day."

Tess cocked her head sideways. "So, micromanagement?"

"No," Alex shot back. "It's transparency. You're already doing the work. This just makes it visible. If you're going to finish the API connector today, you say, 'I commit to finishing the API connector by the end of the day.' If you're going to clear two bugs, you say, 'I'll clear these two bugs today.' And at the next Daily Scrum, you let us know whether you met your commitment and what you accomplished."

"What If?"

Ravi's chair squeaked as he leaned forward, squinting like he'd spotted something on the horizon. "And what happens if we don't finish it?"

49

Alex turned and pointed directly at Tess. "If you say, 'I'm going to finish the API today,' then at tomorrow's Daily Scrum, we ask, 'Did you finish it?' If you did, we celebrate."

Tess tilted her head. "And if I'm wrong? If I miss it?"

"Then we talk about it.," Alex said, repeating the phrase slowly. "Not to blame. Not to shame. The goal is to learn. What happened? Was something blocking you that we didn't see? Did you overcommit? Did priorities shift? We learn, and we get better." Alex shifted her gaze to the whole group. "If you don't finish, it's a conversation. Not a court case."

"Sounds like a court case," Tess muttered.

Ravi smirked, eyes darting to Tess as if they'd just become teammates in rebellion. "So, if I say I'll finish a bug and I don't, I must 'explain myself' in front of the whole team?"

"No one's on trial," Alex said, arms open like they were welcoming a conversation. "This is about clarity, not punishment."

Tess snorted a laugh, not even bothering to hide it. "Sounds like punishment to me."

Stuff Happens

Silence. The kind that hums like feedback from a speaker. Alex knew this moment well. It was the silence that comes after asking people to change. Not just what they do—but how they think about what they do.

"I don't like it," Tess said finally. She leaned forward, placing both hands on her knees like she was about to make a closing argument. "Here's why. Stuff happens during the day. New bugs, new blockers, random requests from Kira."

"Hey," Kira said on the conference screen, offended. "I don't make random requests."

"You know what I mean," Tess said, waving her off. "Point is, we already pivot every few hours. So, if I say, 'I'll finish Task X today,' but then three more urgent things hit my plate, I fail. Then what? I explain myself to the team like I failed a test?"

Alex nodded, listening carefully. "I hear you. But that's not how this works." She took a slow step forward, speaking slowly, clearly. "If a high-priority task hits mid-day, you just say that. 'I committed to X, but Y came in, and Y took priority.' No guilt. No shame. Just reality."

Tess squinted. "You're saying we can change our commitments?"

"Of course," Alex replied. "Commitments are living things, not contracts. The point is to be clear and honest about what's happening."

Tess didn't respond. She sat back slowly, eyes narrowed, calculating.

"We're already doing commitments," Tess said, flicking her hand toward the board. "We have sprint goals. That's commitment."

"Sprint goals aren't commitments," Alex said, motioning supportively toward her. "They're desired outcomes. Aspirations. Intentions. Commitments are different."

Ravi sat up, eyes curious now. "Different how?"

Alex drew a line on the board. "Sprint goals happen once. Commitments are clear, specific promises to deliver measurable progress. Commitments happen every day." She underlined the words every day three times.

"Every day, at Daily Scrum," Alex continued, "each of us will say one thing we'll get done by the end of the day. Not 'I'm working on it.' Not 'I'm looking into it.' I'm talking about something you can measure. Something you can say, 'I did it. Here's the proof.'"

Ravi rubbed his chin, staring at the whiteboard. "So, we call it out every day, huh? Put it on record?"

"Yep," Alex said. "No hiding."

"Brutal," Ravi muttered.

"Brutal, but fair," Alex replied. "Here's the secret, though. Once you get good at this, you'll start doing it automatically. It becomes a micro-habit. You start thinking, 'What can I actually finish today?' instead of 'What can I start?'"

Ravi gave a slow nod. "I like that."

Tess, however, didn't look convinced.

Lowballing

"I'll tell you what's going to happen," Tess said, arms folded. "We're all going to lowball it. We're going to say, 'I'll fix one bug,' so we can always succeed. No one's going to stretch."

"Maybe at first, yeah," Alex admitted, giving a small nod. "But something funny happens. People don't like doing less than they're capable of. It eats at you. When you see Ravi say, 'I'm fixing three bugs,' you'll want to say four. Not because anyone tells you to, but because it's how we're wired. We don't like being the weak link."

Ravi smiled, his eyes shifting to Tess. "Sounds like you're worried I'm going to outwork you, Tess."

Tess's eyes flashed. "Not a chance, QA."

Alex caught the spark. That was the seed. She didn't have to win the whole team today. She just had to plant the seed.

"What's the Point?"

Ravi shifted his head, pointing his pen at Alex like a dart. "Okay, but what's the point?"

Alex exhaled slowly. "Because right now, we're hiding."

The team stared at her. Tess blinked. Ravi sat forward.

"Right now," Alex continued, "we all give updates like this: 'I'm working on it,' 'I'm blocked,' 'I'm doing stuff.' But no one knows what that actually means. It's vague. It's slippery. It's easy to hide."

Alex stepped forward, closer to the group now. "Commitments make it clear. Here's what I did yesterday. Here's what I'm doing today. Here's where I'm stuck. No hiding."

Called Out

"Alright," Tess said, arms folded, tilting her chair back. "I'll play. But I want to hear your commitment first, boss."

Her eyes locked on Alex like a challenge.

Ravi's eyebrows shot up. He leaned forward, grinning. "Yeah, yeah. Put your money where your mouth is, Alex."

Alex hesitated for half a second. The room was still.

Then, with slow, deliberate clarity, Alex spoke. "Here's my commitment."

The weight of her own words hit harder than expected. Her mind scrambled. If she over-committed, Tess would call her on it. If she under-committed, it would look weak. No escape. No exit. No hiding.

"Today, I'll finalize the Daily Scrum structure," Alex said, eyes sharp now. "By 4 p.m., I'll write and share a new format that we'll use for the next two sprints. I'll also review our current board and remove any old, stale tickets."

Silence.

Ravi blinked. "Okay," he said, scratching his chin. "That was... clear."

Tess leaned forward, her eyes locked on Alex. "Fine. I'll commit, too." She glanced at her screen. "Today, I'll finish the API integration. No half-done excuses this time. End of day, it's done."

"Awesome," Alex said, giving her a nod.

The Next Day

The Daily Scrum was different the next day. Alex stood at the front, marker in hand. The whiteboard was split into two columns: "Today's Commitments" on the left, "Tomorrow's Results" on the right.

The rule was simple. At today's Daily Scrum, each person declared at least one specific thing they would complete before the next Daily Scrum. Tomorrow, they would either mark it as, DONE or NOT DONE, with a short explanation. No excuses. No fluff. No "working on it."

Ravi's Turn

"Ravi, you're up," Alex said, marker ready.

Ravi sat back, rubbing his chin. He glanced at Tess, smirked, and leaned forward. "I'll fix three bugs. By end of day, I'll have three ready for verification."

Alex smiled and wrote it down. "Three bugs. Done."

Tess's Turn

"Tess, your turn," Alex prompted.

Tess leaned back in her chair, arms crossed, her sharp gaze sweeping across the room as if calculating how far to test the waters. "First off," she began, her tone even but edged with defiance, "I did finish the API integration yesterday." She paused, watching for any reaction.

"That's fantastic!" Kira exclaimed on screen, her enthusiasm cutting through the tension like sunlight breaking through clouds.

"Well done," Alex affirmed.

Tess pressed on, her voice steady and deliberate, as though Kira's praise and Alex's affirmation hadn't reached her. "Today, I'll finish the login logic by 5 p.m. No excuses this time."

Alex nodded, a faint smile playing at the corners of her lips and jotted on the board: "Finish login logic."

Nia's Turn

Alex looked to Nia next. "Nia, what's your commitment for today?"

Nia hesitated as she tapped her pen against her desk. "Uh...I'll finish reviewing the pull requests for the billing module and merge the clean ones by 2 p.m."

Alex smiled. "Great."

Ethan's Turn

Next was Ethan. He leaned back in his chair, his usual slouch a little more pronounced. "I'll finish the analytics story and push it to staging by end of day."

"Okay," Alex said, making a note on the whiteboard. "And what's the first step you'll take?"

Ethan shrugged, then caught Alex's expectant look. "Uh... I'll try to finalize the dataset by 11 a.m. and review the UI updates after that."

The vague wording didn't slip past Alex. "Hey Ethan, there was one word in that commitment that undermined it. I'm not sure you even realized it."

"What word?" Ethan asked inquisitively.

Ravi spoke up immediately, "Try!"

Ethan paused for a moment and then modified his commitment, "I *will* finalize the dataset by 11 a.m. and review the UI updates after that."

"Super," Alex said with a small smile.

Mateo's Turn

Mateo followed, sitting upright and looking slightly uncomfortable. "I'll review the error logs for the payment gateway bug and write one test case for it by lunch time."

"Thanks, Mateo," Alex said. "Clear and actionable. I like it."

Amina's Turn

Amina, sitting two chairs away, nodded thoughtfully before her turn. "I'll automate the test cases for the notifications module and deploy them to the QA environment before the end of the day."

"Perfect" Alex said, jotting it down.

Harper's Turn

Harper spoke next, "I'll finish the test design for the user profile page by 3 p.m."

Alex made eye contact. "Sounds good. Is there anything you anticipate needing help with?"

Harper shook her head. "No, I think I'm okay."

Sofia's Turn

Sofia straightened in her seat, a hint of determination in her tone. "I commit to completing the API documentation for the user permissions service and get it reviewed by 4 p.m."

"That's a strong commitment, Sofia," Alex said, marking it on the board.

Liam's Turn

Finally, Alex turned to Liam. He sat at the edge of the table, arms crossed and clearly skeptical. He had been quiet throughout the meeting, his usual demeanor tinged with visible doubt.

"Liam, what's your commitment for today?" Alex asked, keeping her tone encouraging.

Liam leaned back, exhaling sharply. "Fine. I'll refactor the login service."

Alex didn't write it down right away. "What's the first thing you'll tackle to get there?"

Liam glanced around, his expression impatient. "Uh…I'll review the logs and isolate the timeout conditions by noon."

"Good," Alex said, writing his commitment on the board. "If anything comes up, don't hesitate to reach out."

Liam gave a short nod, but his eyes stayed on the board, scanning the commitments. Alex could sense the resistance softening, just a little.

Kira's Turn

"Kira?" Alex called out. Her face appeared again on the conference screen.

"I'll clear the top five unrefined backlog items," Kira said confidently. "I'll get them ready for refinement this afternoon."

"Five backlog items," Alex repeated, writing it down. "Clear it. Lock it in."

The Following Day

The next day, Alex opened the Daily Scrum with a recap of the team's first commitments.

"Ravi," Alex called out, marker ready. "Three bugs. Did you do it?"

"Done," Ravi grinned, thumping his chest twice and miming a mic drop. "Three verified. Check Jira."

Alex grinned, turning to the board. "Done." She underlined it. Tess glanced at Ravi but didn't say anything.

"Tess," Alex said, turning toward her. "Login logic. Done?"

Tess hesitated for half a second, then nodded slowly. "Yeah. Done."

"Say it with heart, Tess," Ravi said, smiling.

Tess smirked. "Done."

Alex smiled and wrote "done" on the board.

The other engineers reviewed their commitments, too. Nia completed her pull request reviews, earning a quick round of nods from the group as she explained how she streamlined the code. Ethan admitted he hadn't finished the analytics chart, citing unexpected issues with the dataset. "What was learned from that?" Alex asked, turning the miss into an opportunity for reflection. Harper shared that she completed the test design, smiling as the team acknowledged her effort with encouraging words. Mateo reported clear progress on error log tasks but said he needed more time to write the test case for the payment gateway bug. Mateo recommitted to the test case. Amina finished the unit tests, prompting Alex to highlight how her work increased quality. Sofia wrapped up her API documentation as promised, earning quiet but visible respect from the group. Liam, to everyone's surprise, had not only refactored the login service but also resolved a secondary issue. Alex made sure to call out his extra effort, saying, "Great work, Liam. Thanks for going the extra mile."

Then Alex turned to Kira, "Kira, you had five backlog items to clear. Did you do it?"

Kira hesitated, biting her lip. "Only got three done. I had a last-minute meeting with Nathan."

"Three out of five," Alex said, still writing. "Not done, but we know why."

"Yeah," Kira said. "Next time, I'll leave buffer room."

No court case. No chastising. No punishment.

The Shift Begins

Over the next week, everything changed slowly, but visibly. At first, Tess rolled her eyes every time she had to state her commitment.

But on Thursday, she finished a story she'd been dragging for weeks. There was a sense of relief. She didn't say it out loud, but Alex saw it in her face.

Ravi started treating his commitments like a game. "I'll crush three bugs by 4 p.m.," he said with a grin during the Daily Scrum on Friday. He cleared four. Tess clapped. Others cheered.

On Friday, Kira was the last to give her commitment. She rubbed her eyes like she'd been staring at the screen for too long. "I'll clear the backlog of unrefined stories today," she said with a sigh. "At least six of them."

"Seven," Tess said. "You can do seven." Others agreed.

Kira glanced at her, surprised, but then smiled. "Seven it is."

Chapter 4 Summary

In Chapter 4, Alex introduces Commitment Language as the first step in the F.I.T. Formula, transforming vague updates into specific, actionable daily commitments. The team, initially resistant, begins to embrace accountability, specificity, and transparency through small, incremental accomplishments.

Key Developments

1. **Introducing Commitment Language**
   - Alex proposes measurable daily commitments during Daily Scrums, replacing vague updates like "I'm working on it."
   - Commitments are revisited in the next Daily Scrum, and marked as either DONE or NOT DONE, followed by a brief explanation.
   - The new format introduces a whiteboard update with two new columns: "Today's Commitments" and "Tomorrow's Results."

- Alex predicts that the team will naturally push themselves to achieve more once they see others succeeding.

2. **Resistance to Change**
   - Tess and Ravi's skepticism reflects the natural resistance teams face when asked to change established habits and mindsets.
   - Tess and Ravi resist, citing shifting priorities and fear of judgment. Tess accuses Alex of "micromanagement."

3. **Alex's Leadership**
   - Alex frames the shift as a move toward transparency and action, not blame or punishment.
   - Alex exhibits effective leadership by addressing their concerns calmly and showing empathy.
   - Alex demonstrates the change by making her own public commitment, diffusing tension and earning trust. This inspires the team to cautiously adopt the practice.

4. **Commitment Review**
   - At the next day's Daily Scrum, the team reviews their commitments:
     1. Ravi completed three bugs as promised.
     2. Tess delivered the login logic she committed to finishing.
     3. Nia completed the pull request reviews.
     4. Ethan ran into an unexpected dataset issue but learned from it.
     5. Harper completed her test design as pledged.
     6. Mateo missed his commitment to finish the test case for the payment gateway bug and recommitted to in the Daily Scrum.
     7. Amina finished the unit tests she committed to complete.
     8. Sofia wrapped up her API documentation as promised.
     9. Liam refactored the login service and resolved a secondary issue.
     10. Kira cleared three out of five backlog items but openly explained why she fell short.

- The team begins to see the value of public commitments and transparent, blame-free accountability.
- These early successes build trust and create positive momentum.

Key Concepts

1. **Commitment Language for Accountability and Transparency**
   - Replaces vague updates with clear, actionable commitments that prioritize measurable progress over ambiguous effort.
   - Encourages team members to critically assess their daily priorities, fostering specificity and clarity about what needs to get done.
   - The shift from "doing tasks" to "making promises" builds visible accountability and transparency, aligning individual contributions with team goals.
   - Commitments are made public during the Daily Scrum, reinforcing follow-through and creating shared understanding.

2. **Micro-Habits for Sustainable Productivity**
   - Daily commitments instill a mindset shift from "What can I start today?" to "What can I finish today?" prioritizing progress over activity.
   - Over time, these habits drive consistent individual and team productivity, embedding a culture of steady, incremental progress.
   - Accountability Without Blame
   - Missed commitments are reframed as opportunities to learn, fostering psychological safety and building a culture of constructive feedback and improvement.

Themes and Takeaways

1. **The Challenge of Change**
   - Resistance is natural in any transformation. Leaders must listen, address concerns empathetically, and model the desired behaviors to build trust and guide their teams through uncertainty.

2. **The Benefits of Daily Micro-Commitments with Commitment Language**
   - **Clarity and Focus**
     - **Clarity**: Establishes clear, actionable goals, reducing ambiguity and aligning priorities.
     - **Focus**: Promotes a "done" mindset by prioritizing task completion over starting new work.
   - **Trust and Accountability**
     - **Accountability**: Encourages personal ownership as individuals commit publicly and deliver on promises.
     - **Trust-Building**: Fosters reliability and team cohesion as members consistently follow through.
   - **Collaboration and Adaptability**
     - **Collaboration**: Aligns individual efforts with team objectives, ensuring shared success.
     - **Adaptability**: Enables teams to adjust commitments daily in response to changing priorities or challenges.
   - **Momentum and Psychological Safety**
     - **Momentum**: Creates a virtuous cycle of small wins that build confidence and motivation.
     - **Psychological Safety**: Encourages open discussions of progress and obstacles without fear of blame.
   - **Efficiency and Skill Development**
     - **Reduced Cognitive Load**: Breaks work into manageable tasks, preventing overload and enabling better decisions.

- **Skill Development**: Builds habits of prioritization, communication, and follow-through, enhancing individual and team capabilities.

3. **The Power of Small Wins**
   - Incremental successes, celebrated openly, build momentum, strengthen team morale, and reinforce new behaviors, creating a foundation for long-term success.

Conclusion

Chapter 4 captures the initial resistance and gradual adoption of Commitment Language within Team Swaggernauts. Through empathy, clear leadership, and small wins, Alex sets the foundation for a team culture rooted in accountability and transparency.

Reflection Questions

- How clear and actionable are your commitments to your team, and how do you hold yourself accountable?
- What specific behaviors could you adopt to better model desired behavior?

Chapter 5

Fractals in Focus:
Redefining Team Success

"I'm not doing it."

Tess's voice was sharp and clear, like the clang of a dropped wrench in a silent garage. She sat back in her chair, arms crossed, eyes daring anyone to challenge her.

"Not doing what?" Alex asked, already knowing where this was going.

Tess pointed at the whiteboard at the front of the room. Two large words were written in bold black letters: "Dynamic Fractals."

"We're not breaking into mini-teams," Tess said firmly. "I'm a developer. I write code. I don't need to be on some 'fractal' to do it."

"You're missing the point," Alex replied, forcing calm into her voice. "This isn't about being in 'fractals.' It's about structure for collaboration and focus."

"I'm already focused," Tess shot back. She pointed to her monitor. "I'm focusing on this API right now. Guess what I don't need? Two other people standing over my shoulder."

The room felt tense. Ravi glanced up from his notebook, shifting in his chair like he was watching a tennis match. All he needed was some movie theater popcorn to watch the show.

Kira, dialed in on the conference screen, had her head down, typing furiously on her keyboard but clearly listening.

Taking a prescriptive Shu stance, "This isn't optional," Alex said kindly but firmly. "We're trying something new to meet Nathan's deadline. That said, I truly believe this will help the team and I'm asking you to trust me. Commitment Language provided visible progress in our first sprint, yet fourteen of the fifteen critical features remain unfinished. We need more focus and follow-through in Sprint Two."

"Trying something new," Tess repeated, throwing her hands in the air. "Translation: More process. More meetings. More 'team-building experiments.' We've done this before, Alex. It never works."

Ravi smirked. "She's got a point."

"This is different," Alex said, stepping forward. "This isn't just 'more process.' It's about structure and getting work done faster, with less confusion and less blame." Alex's eyes scanned the room. "We've all seen what happens when stories get stuck. Everyone points fingers, and no one takes ownership. Dynamic Fractals change that."

Tess raised her eyebrows. "How?"

"By making smaller, tighter delivery units," Alex explained. "Instead of nine people independently working on nine or more stories at once in a larger team, we have small fractals of three people focused on one story at a time. No handoffs. No 'It's not my part.' If you're in the fractal, you finish the story, together. Period."

Tess leaned forward, resting her arms on her knees. "And what happens if the other team needs me for something else? You gonna clone me, Alex?"

"No," Alex replied. "Because you won't be working on five stories at once anymore. You'll be working on one."

The room went still.

"One story at a time," Tess repeated slowly, her words deliberate, as if she were testing their weight, letting the idea settle into the air around her.

"For real?"

"For real," Alex replied. "That's why we're doing WIP Limits too."

Kira, still on video, leaned forward. "I like it," she said. "If it means fewer half-done stories, I'm in."

"Of course you like it," Tess said, glancing at the screen. "You're not the one doing the work."

"Oh, come on, Tess," Kira shot back. "I've been in every sprint review where we show up with five 'almost-done' features and no actual releases. It's embarrassing. We need something different."

The Split

"Here's what it looks like," Alex said, walking to the whiteboard. She drew three small circles inside a larger circle.

Fractal A → Tess (Software Engineer) + Ravi (QA Engineer) + Amina (Software Engineer)
Fractal B → Liam (Software Engineer) + Sofia (Software Engineer) + Mateo (QA Engineer)
Fractal C → Nia (Software Engineer) + Ethan (Software Engineer) + Harper (QA Engineer)

"We're forming three fractals," Alex said, circling each small group. "Three people per fractal. Each fractal focuses on one story at a time. Only one."

Tess raised her hand slowly, still looking at the board. "Okay, so you want me to work on one story. With Ravi. All day."

"Correct. And Amina."

Amina, the newest member of the team, sat quietly, her pen poised over her notebook. A junior developer with a brilliant mind, Amina was still finding her footing in the chaos of Daily Scrums. Her academic background—filled with clear expectations and measurable goals—had prepared her to excel, but the messy reality of a Scrum team was something else entirely. She wanted to contribute, to prove herself, but the louder personalities around her often overshadowed her voice.

Gathering courage, "I really like the idea of fractals," Amina said with a shy smile. "It feels like I'll have more chances to learn from everyone, and I won't feel so alone trying to figure things out by myself."

Tess leaned back, tapping her fingers on the desk. "What if Ravi and Amina don't keep up?"

"Then you help them," Alex replied. "Because you're in a fractal together. It's not 'one person's problem' anymore. It's your problem together."

Ravi twisted his head. "What if Tess decides I'm the slow one and throws me under the bus?"

"She won't," Alex said. "Because you'll be finishing the story together. It's not her story. It's not your story. It's not Amina's story. It's your fractal's story. If it fails, it fails together."

"Fail together," Tess muttered, shaking her head like it was a bad punchline.

"Or win together," Alex said firmly, eyes on Tess. "That's your call."

One Modification

"Wait, one more thing," Alex said, pausing with a hint of excitement. "Once you start working in fractals, the way you use Commitment Language changes."

"Changes how?" Ravi asked, curiosity sparking in his voice.

"Well," Alex began, leaning forward, "since you succeed or fail as a fractal, commitments shift from individual promises to collective commitments."

Tess raised an eyebrow. "You mean one shared commitment for me, Ravi, and Amina?"

"Exactly," Alex replied with a nod. "You commit as a fractal— how you get it done is up to you. It's about collective effort, not just individual pieces."

Ravi glanced at Tess and Amina, considering it. "So, we're aligning upfront, not just scrambling during the day?"

"Exactly!" Alex said, tapping the whiteboard for emphasis. "Here's a tip: before the Daily Scrum, huddle up as a fractal. Sync up on what you accomplished yesterday and what you'll commit to today. That way, you're walking in with a unified plan."

Tess leaned back, a thoughtful smile forming. "That actually makes a lot of sense. It's like…we're committing to win together."

Alex grinned. "Bingo. One fractal, one commitment, one win."

The First Day

The first day with the new structure was chaos.

"Where's Ravi?" Tess asked, looking around, clearly irritated. "He's supposed to be here for this API integration. I'm not doing it alone."

"Relax, I'm here," Ravi said, jogging over with a bag of chips in his hand. He dropped into his chair, munching loudly. "What's the crisis?"

"The crisis is you eating chips while Amina and I wait for you to help with the database calls," Tess snapped. "We've been here for twenty minutes."

Alex watched from afar, not stepping in. She knew this was part of it.

Dynamic Fractals don't succeed on day one. They succeed on day six, or ten, or twenty. People aren't used to sharing responsibility like this.

By day three of the sprint, Tess, Ravi, and Amina's fractal was arguing less. The lines between "developer work" and "QA work" blurred. On day four, they completed a story, getting it done faster than expected.

By Friday, something unexpected happened.

"Hey, Tess, how do you write your API tests?" Ravi asked, leaning toward her.

Tess blinked, visibly stunned. "You want to know about API tests?"

"Yeah," Ravi said, grinning. "If I'm stuck here on your team, I might as well learn something."

Alex watched the whole thing from a distance, pretending to check her notes but smiling so wide it almost hurt.

Winning

On the following Wednesday, Alex gathered the team for a retro. "Alright, let's retro. One sprint down. What went well?"

Tess raised a hand slowly. "I'll say it. Fractals kinda work."

Alex blinked, genuinely surprised. "Really?"

Tess shrugged. "Don't make it weird, Alex."

Ravi grinned, arms folded. "They work 'cause I'm awesome."

"No," Tess said, deadpan. "They work 'cause we're forced to finish. No more 'that's your part, this is my part.' It's just us. If I mess up, I mess it up for him. So, I stop messing up."

Alex nodded slowly. "Win together. Fail together."

"Yeah," Tess said. "But I prefer winning."

Chapter 5 Summary

In Chapter 5, Alex introduces Dynamic Fractals and WIP Limits as transformative practices to Team Swaggernauts. By restructuring the team into smaller fractals, each focused on one story at a time, the chapter captures the challenges of resistance, the initial chaos, and the eventual success that signals the start of cultural change.

Key Developments

1. **The Introduction of Dynamic Fractals and WIP Limits**
    -   Alex divides the team into three smaller fractals of three members each, emphasizing collective ownership over stories. These are fixed fractals initially.

- Fractals adhere to a WIP Limit of one story at a time.
- This structural change shifts the team's approach from individual contributions to shared responsibility.
- Commitment Language evolves to reflect shared accountability within fractals.

2. **Resistance to Change**
   - Tess questions the necessity of fractals, while Ravi raises concerns about dependencies.
   - Alex reframes the change as a way to focus, build ownership, and remove blame.
   - Amina, a junior developer, is optimistic about the potential for collaboration and learning.

3. **Chaotic Beginnings**
   - The initial days of implementation are marked by tension and adjustment.
   - Despite early friction, fractals begin working together, with Tess and Ravi finding common ground by the third day.

4. **Early Successes**
   - Tess and Ravi collaborate on API testing, demonstrating the potential for cross-training and mutual respect.
   - The team experiences its first tangible win under the new system, bolstering morale and belief in the process.
   - This collaboration also represents the team's first tangible success under the new system, signaling the potential for long-term cultural change.

5. **Momentum Through Small Wins**
   - By the end of the sprint, Tess acknowledges the value of Dynamic Fractals and WIP Limits, albeit reluctantly.
   - The team recognizes the benefits of shared accountability, with fewer incomplete stories and greater focus.

Key Concepts

1. **Dynamic Fractals for Collaboration and Responsibility**
   - Small, three-person team structures foster real-time collaboration, seamless communication, and shared responsibility for outcomes, ensuring collective ownership of tasks.
   - Full fractal responsibility eliminates silos, reduces finger-pointing, and builds trust by emphasizing shared successes and learning from collective failures.

2. **WIP Limits for Focus and Quality**
   - By working on a single story at a time, fractals minimize context switching, enabling deep focus and consistent progress.
   - This limitation fosters steady delivery, faster task completion, and higher-quality outcomes.

3. **Commitment Language Modification for Shared Accountability**
   - Shifting from individual to fractal commitments aligns team efforts with collective goals, reinforcing shared accountability and cohesion.

Themes and Takeaways

1. **Navigating Resistance to Change**
   Change requires empathetic leadership, clear communication, and persistent belief in the team's ability to succeed. In challenging moments, leaders must combine kindness with firmness to guide the team through uncertainty.

2. **The Benefits of Dynamic Fractals and WIP Limits**
   - **Collaboration and Trust**
     - **Skill-Sharing**: Encourages cross-functional learning and enhances team expertise.
     - **Trust-Building**: Reinforces deep connections through collective accountability and shared outcomes.

- **Collaboration**: Breaks down silos, enabling smoother communication and stronger alignment.
- **Efficiency and Quality**
  - **Efficiency**: Eliminates handoffs and context-switching, ensuring faster delivery.
  - **Higher Quality**: Focusing on one story at a time reduces errors and ensures better results.
  - **Engagement**: Active participation boosts morale and motivation.
- **Adaptability and Innovation**
  - **Resilience**: Cohesive decision-making enables teams to adapt quickly to challenges.
  - **Innovation**: Diverse perspectives spark creative problem-solving and drive innovation.
- **Accountability and Ownership**
  - **Accountability**: Aligns effort with clear goals and outcomes, fostering collective responsibility and follow-through.
  - **Ownership**: Encourages self-organization and pride in progress by enabling teams to manage their flow and focus together.

Conclusion

Chapter 5 chronicles the team's first use of Dynamic Fractals and WIP Limits in sprint two, revealing their initial challenges and gradual breakthroughs. The narrative illustrates how structural changes can catalyze cultural transformation, fostering new ways of thinking and working. This chapter further emphasizes the critical role of persistence, collaboration, and shared responsibility in driving sustainable team success.

Reflection Questions

- How might smaller, more focused groups improve your team's ability to deliver value collaboratively?
- What behaviors do you notice in yourself or others that contribute to shared ownership of tasks?

Chapter 6

Teaming to Success:
Collaboration Unleashed

The Problem No One Saw Coming

It started with a big red "blocked" label on the board. It was Sprint Three and twelve of fifteen critical features lingered.

The words were sharp and angry in bold, red letters, plastered on a Jira ticket that sat dead in the middle of Team Swaggernauts' Kanban board. Story #172: "Enable Customer Payment Gateway."

That story was supposed to be "in progress" for two days. Now it had been blocked for four. No movement. No commits. No updates. Just stalled.

"We need to talk about this," Alex said during the next Daily Scrum. She tapped the card on the board with the tip of a marker. "Story #172. What's going on?"

Tess didn't even look up from her keyboard. "Ravi needs to run the regression tests before I push the final build."

Ravi, sitting directly across from her, narrowed his eyes. "No, no, no. I already ran the tests. Twice. Your API call still fails half the time."

"Then you ran it wrong," Tess said flatly, typing even faster. "It's not my call that's broken."

"It is your call, Tess," Ravi shot back, raising his voice now. "You wrote the logic. I'm not a mind reader. I don't know how it's supposed to work if you don't tell me."

Their fierce exchange made it clear to Alex that despite working in fractals, limiting WIP, and making collective commitments, they were still operating as individuals.

Off to the side, Amina sat watching the fireworks, distress etched across her face. Alex then glanced over at Kira, who had dialed in for the Daily Scrum. Her face was a picture of concern, her lips pursed in silent disapproval. Everyone could feel it.

"Pause," Alex said, stepping forward, palms out. "We're not doing this today." She walked to the whiteboard and circled the big red "blocked" label. "We're not pointing fingers. We're fixing this. Together. Now."

The Concept of Mobbing

Alex gripped the whiteboard marker like a conductor ready to command an orchestra. "I threw you into Dynamic Fractals and WIP Limits expecting you to just 'figure it out.' No real guidance. No framework for how to work together. That was my mistake."

Alex took a breath. "Listen up; new concept. The fractal is Mobbing this. Right now."

Tess raised her eyebrows. "Mobbing?"

"Yeah," Alex replied, stepping to the center of the room. "Everyone in the fractal on the same problem at the same time. No split focus. No silos. We solve it together."

Tess tilted her head, skeptical. "So, you're telling me, instead of doing our own jobs, we all do mine?"

"No, we do ours." Alex's eyes moved from Tess to Ravi to Amina. "This is the fractal's problem. The whole fractal owns the blocker. Tess, you drive. Ravi, you co-pilot. Amina, you observe. I'll facilitate."

"Pass," Tess muttered. "Not happening."

"It's happening," Alex said, stepping closer. "You've been stuck on this for four days, Tess. Four. Days. What's the plan? Do we wait for day five? Day six? Or do we solve it today?"

The room fell silent.

Ravi tapped his pen against his notepad, glanced at Tess, then shrugged. "I'm in."

Alex raised a hand. "All in favor of Mobbing this blocker right now, raise your hand."

Ravi raised his hand immediately. Amina, glancing at Ravi, raised her hand. Kira, still on video, raised a hand onscreen.

Tess sat still, arms crossed.

"Don't be stubborn, Tess," Kira said through the screen. "We need this done."

Tess rolled her eyes and raised her hand. "Fine. Mob it."

The Mob

"Alright," Alex said, feeling momentum build. "Here's how we do it."

The Driver: Tess takes control of the shared screen. One keyboard. One screen.

The Navigator: Ravi offers guidance, provides data, and cross-checks everything Tess does.

The Observer: Amina, if you see something, say something. No silent onlookers.

"Everyone ready?" Alex asked.

Ravi leaned forward. "Let's fly."

Amina said, "Let's do it!"

Ten Minutes In

Tess shared her screen. The screen lit up with the VS Code editor, a wall of blue, green, and white text. She scrolled to the section of the API call that handled error responses from the payment gateway.

"Right here," she said, tapping a highlighted line. "This should catch the response code from the payment API. If it's a 400 or 500, it retries automatically."

"Retries?" Ravi squinted. "That's weird. Why would it retry on a 400? That's a bad request, not a server issue."

Tess paused. Her fingers hovered over the keyboard. Her eyes flicked left, then right.

"Yeah, but it's supposed to retry," she said, defensive now. "That's how it's supposed to work."

"No, Tess, a 400 means we screwed up. You only retry on a 500." Ravi leaned forward, pointing at the line of code. "You're retrying requests that are already bad."

Tess's lips pressed into a hard line. Her eyes stayed on the screen.

"Change it," Ravi said. "No point retrying a bad request."

Tess didn't move.

"Just try it, Tess," Amina said. "What if it works?"

Tess groaned, and with two furious keystrokes, she commented out the logic for retrying 400-level errors.

"Alright," she muttered. "Run it."

Ravi's fingers flew across his own keyboard, pulling up the regression test suite.

They all watched.

> Test 1... Pass.
> Test 2... Pass.
> Test 3... Pass.

"Huh," Tess muttered, slouching back in her chair humbled. "Guess that was it."

Ravi grinned. "Told you."

"Don't get cocky, QA," Tess said, but her voice was softer now.

The Surprise

That first mob session ended with an unexpected result.

They liked it.

"Hey," Tess said, glancing over at Ravi. "That was actually faster than I thought."

"Yeah," Ravi said, still scrolling through the test results. "We should do this more."

"Glad you said that," Alex said, smiling. "Because tomorrow, we're doing a Swarming session."

Tess groaned. "What now?"

"Swarming," Alex said, tapping the whiteboard. "Whole fractal, multiple keyboards, one story. We're all working on one story together, step by step, side by side."

"That sounds like overkill," Tess muttered.

Alex shrugged. "We'll see."

The Next Day: The Swarming Experiment

"Okay," Alex said, still feeling the rush of energy from the previous day. "Here's how we swarm."

Align: As a fractal, align on the approach to deliver. Adjust as necessary.

Multiple Drivers: Everyone works simultaneously on their own laptop.

Multiple Tasks: Only one story, but multiple, concurrent tasks for that one story.

Shared Space: The fractal sits together and communicates and collaborates in real-time.

Help: If one member gets stuck, pair off or mob it as a fractal.

"Good to go?" Alex asked.

Ravi smiled. "Swarm, baby, swarm."

"You bet!" said Amina.

Even Tess was on board. "Let's give it a whirl."

Ravi, Tess, and Amina huddled together in a corner of the team space, their laptops open and humming as they swarmed on a new story.

Tess quickly outlined the approach, her fingers flying over the keyboard as she set up the initial framework.

Next to her, Ravi leaned in, offering suggestions and pairing briefly with Amina to debug a tricky part of the integration.

Amina, energized by the collaboration, tackled the unit tests, her confidence growing with every passing minute.

Tess, Ravi, and Amina would sync regularly, often out loud and sometimes pausing, sharing their progress and pivoting as needed. The rhythm of their work was smooth and focused.

In just a few hours, the story moved from "In Progress" to "Done," and as Amina pushed the final commit, a satisfied grin spread across her face.

"That was fast," Ravi said, leaning back.

Tess nodded, adding, "Swarming for the win."

Another Mobbing Experiment

The following day, the fractal gathered in front of a single, shared screen, taking turns controlling the keyboard.

One driver. One navigator. One observer. Everyone leaned in, rotating. They worked on a thorny bug that had haunted them for two sprints. It took forty-five minutes.

Forty-five minutes.

Tess looked at the time and shook her head, laughing. "I spent two days on that bug last sprint. Two whole days."

"And you could have fixed it in forty-five minutes," Kira added.

"Not me—us," Tess said, glancing at the fractal. "We fixed it."

Chapter 6 Summary

In Chapter 6, Alex introduces Mobbing and Swarming to tackle critical blockers and enhance collaboration. These Teaming techniques shift the team from isolated work to collective problem-solving, driving efficiency and building trust.

Key Developments

1. **Unblocking the Gateway**
   - Story #172, "Enable Customer Payment Gateway," remains stuck for four days, escalating tension between Tess and Ravi.
   - Alex intervenes to halt the blame game, redirecting focus toward a collaborative solution.

2. **Mobbing Session**
   - Alex initiates Mobbing, assigning Tess as the driver, Ravi as co-pilot, and Amina as an observer.
   - The team uncovers and fixes a logic flaw in Tess's API code, resolving the blocker and passing regression tests.
   - Another Mobbing session resolves a bug in just forty-five minutes, a task that previously took two days.
   - By pooling their skills and knowledge, the team overcomes challenges that individual efforts could not.

3. **Swarming Session**
   - Alex builds on the Mobbing success by introducing Swarming, where the team collaborates on one story, completing multiple tasks simultaneously.
   - The team finishes a story in hours, showcasing the power of unified effort.

4. **Evolving Dynamics**
   - Tess transitions from skepticism to recognizing the effectiveness of Mobbing and Swarming.
   - Tess's shift in attitude underscores the importance of experiencing success to embrace new methods.
   - The team begins to internalize the idea that blockers and problems are shared responsibilities, moving toward collective accountability and ownership.

Key Concepts

1. **Mobbing for Problem-Solving**
   - A Teaming technique where the entire fractal focuses on resolving a single task or blocker together, leveraging their collective expertise to solve problems quickly and foster cross-functional learning.

2. **Swarming for Story Completion**
   - A Teaming technique where the entire fractal works on a single story at a time, coordinating multiple tasks concurrently to accelerate progress while enhancing team trust and collaboration.

Themes and Takeaways

- **Benefits of Teaming (Mobbing, Swarming, and Pairing)**
  1. **Collaboration and Learning**
     - **Improved Problem-Solving**: Combines diverse perspectives to tackle complex challenges, leading to innovative and effective solutions.
     - **Skill-Sharing**: Facilitates real-time knowledge transfer, enhancing cross-functional capabilities and team growth.
     - **Efficient Onboarding**: Quickly integrates new members by involving them in active collaboration.
  2. **Team Dynamics and Culture**
     - **Psychological Safety**: Builds a safe environment wherein team members feel comfortable contributing and learning without fear of judgment.
     - **Team Bonding**: Strengthens relationships and trust through close collaboration.
     - **Shared Ownership**: Reinforces a "win together, fail together" mindset, fostering collective accountability.

- **Reduces Social Loafing**: Ensures active participation and visible contributions in group settings.

3. **Efficiency and Productivity**
   - **Faster Resolution**: Speeds up task completion by leveraging collective expertise during high-priority situations.
   - **Enhanced Focus**: Concentrates team effort on a single task or problem, reducing distractions and enabling deeper work.
   - **Eliminates Bottlenecks**: Reduces dependencies on single points of expertise, ensuring no one person becomes a blocker.

4. **Quality and Adaptability**
   - **Higher Quality**: Promotes real-time feedback and peer reviews, minimizing errors and ensuring better deliverables.
   - **Adaptability**: Enables teams to pivot quickly in response to changing priorities, leveraging Mobbing and Swarming for dynamic work.
   - **Resilience**: Builds team capacity to handle challenges collectively, making the team less dependent on specific individuals.

Conclusion

Chapter 6 showcases how the Teaming Techniques of Mobbing and Swarming drive efficiency and collaboration. By introducing these techniques, Alex resolves blockers, enhances team cohesion, and sets the foundation for a culture of shared ownership and continuous improvement.

Reflection Questions

- How do you currently respond when a teammate is stuck, and what behavior could you model to foster collaboration?
- What steps can you take to create an environment where seeking help is seen as a strength, not a weakness?

Chapter 7

Breaking Through: Turning Failure into Momentum

The Failure

It happened on a Wednesday during Sprint Four.

Tess was in the middle of a Mobbing session with Ravi, Amina, and Kira, hammering away at the payment validation logic for Project UXcellence. Everything was flowing. Code was being written. Bugs were being squashed. It felt like one of those rare moments of momentum, where every tap of the keyboard pushed them closer to the finish line.

Then it broke.

Not a small break. Not a "fix it in five minutes" break.

It crashed everything.

The API tests went red. The integration tests lit up like a Christmas tree.

Tess froze, fingers hovering over the keys. "What...what just happened?"

Ravi leaned forward, eyes scanning the logs. "Uh... yep. Yep, yep, yep."

"What?" Tess's voice grew sharp.

Ravi glanced at her, his face scrunched with that awkward look people have when they're about to deliver bad news. "The database migration script... It overwrote the old payment tokens." He clicked through the error logs, eyes darting from line to line. "It wiped them."

Tess's heart dropped. "Wiped them?" Her voice went cold. "All of them?"

Ravi tapped one more key, and a number appeared at the bottom of the screen. "All six thousand four hundred eighteen of them."

No one said anything for a moment. The only sound was Tess's shallow breathing. She leaned back in her chair, hands on her head, eyes squeezed shut. "No. No, no, no."

Her chair squeaked as she swiveled to face Ravi. "Why didn't you catch that?"

Ravi jerked his head back. "Me? You wrote the script, Tess!"

"Yeah, but you ran the tests!" Tess shot back. "You're supposed to check for stuff like this."

"How am I supposed to know your script deletes payment tokens, huh?" Ravi's voice rose. "It's not my job to guess your logic!"

"Then what is your job, Ravi?" Tess snapped. "Because it sure isn't catching mistakes."

"Enough!" Alex's voice cut through the room like a whip crack. "Both of you, stop."

Tess turned toward Alex, face flushed red with frustration. "No, Alex. This is on Ravi. He's QA. He's supposed to catch this."

"And you're supposed to test your logic," Alex shot back, her eyes locked on hers. "But I'm not here to point fingers. We're not going to win by blaming each other." She took a step forward, lowering her voice. "We win by learning. Period."

Ravi opened his mouth to respond, but Alex raised a hand, cutting him off.

"We'll deal with it in the retro," Alex said, voice calm but firm. "Right now, we focus. We fix it."

The Crisis

That night, nobody left on time.

The fractal stayed late, working together in a swarm to restore the payment tokens. Every single payment record had to be reloaded. Tess pulled historical backups from the dev server. Ravi ran data integrity checks on every row of data.

By 10:37 p.m., it was done.

Tess leaned back, eyes bloodshot, her face a mix of exhaustion and relief. Ravi threw his head back, letting out a long sigh. Kira's face, still on the conference screen, was practically slumped against her laptop camera.

"Alright, it's fixed," Tess said, eyes closed, head lifted toward the ceiling. She didn't say it with pride. It felt like saying "I'm fine" when you're anything but—necessary, but hollow.

"Cool," Ravi said, his voice hollow too. "Can't wait for that retro tomorrow."

The Retro Begins

Thursday, 9:05 a.m.

The team sat around the conference table, chairs close, eyes tired. Kira's face glowed on the big conference screen. No one was talking.

Alex stood at the front of the room, marker in hand. This retro wasn't going to be easy. It wasn't a normal "how we can do better" session. It was a post-crisis reflection.

Alex drew three columns on the board:

"What went well"
"What didn't go well"
"What we'll do next time"

"Alright, let's start," Alex said, tapping the board. "We all know what happened. No hiding it. The token wipe." She circled "What didn't go well. Let's hear it."

No one spoke. Tess's arms were folded. Ravi stared at the table.

"Ravi," Alex said, looking directly at him. "What didn't go well?"

Ravi hesitated, rubbing the back of his neck. "I missed it," he muttered, eyes still on the table. "I ran the tests and I didn't see it."

Alex nodded. "Okay. That's real. Thank you, Ravi." She wrote it on the board:

"Tests missed database deletion logic."

Alex turned to Tess. "Tess. What didn't go well?"

Tess sighed hard through her nose. "I didn't test it locally before I pushed it." She raised her head back, staring at the ceiling. "I thought it would be fine. It wasn't."

"Okay," Alex said, writing it down: "Code wasn't tested locally before push."

Tess leaned forward, elbows on her knees. Her voice dropped. "That's on me."

Ravi's head snapped up, eyes wide with surprise. He blinked twice, then rubbed his hands together slowly. "Huh."

"What?" Tess asked.

"Nothing," Ravi said, his grin barely contained. "Just didn't expect you to say that."

Tess angled her head toward him, eyes narrowed. "Don't get used to it, QA."

Everyone laughed.

What Went Well

When they got to the "What went well" column, the mood shifted.

"We fixed it fast," Kira said, her face still on the video screen. "Six hours to restore six thousand records is no small feat."

"Yeah," Tess said, sitting up straighter. "Ravi identified the root cause immediately. That could've taken us way longer."

"Agreed," Alex said, writing it down. "Swarming fixed the issue fast."

"Ravi's data integrity checks caught restore errors early. Also," Tess added, looking at Ravi, "we didn't fight as much as usual."

"Don't get used to it," Ravi shot back, grinning.

What We'll Do Next Time

When they got to the "What we'll do next time" column, something changed.

"No more pushing untested migration scripts," Tess said. "If it's data logic, we test it locally. Every time."

Alex nodded. "That's a rule now. I like it."

"I'm adding a regression test for it," Ravi said. "If it happens again, the tests will flag it before it gets to staging."

Alex added it to the board: "New regression tests for destructive actions."

She stood back, arms folded, taking in the board.

"This is the part people miss," Alex said. "This right here. The part where we learn." She circled the "What we'll do next time" column. "If we do this every sprint, we don't just get better. We get unstoppable."

Chapter 7 Summary

Chapter 7 focuses on a critical failure within Team Swaggernauts: an untested migration script deletes over six thousand payment records. The crisis showcases the importance of retrospectives, vulnerability, and collective problem-solving in transforming setbacks into progress.

Key Developments

1. **The Crisis Unfolds**
   - Tess's untested migration script causes significant data loss.
   - The failure triggers tension between Tess and Ravi, threatening team morale.

2. **Collaborative Recovery**
   - Under Alex's guidance, the team swarms late into the night, restoring data within six hours, highlighting their growing collaborative skills.
   - Alex steers the focus away from blame and toward resolution, reinforcing a culture of shared accountability.

3. **The Retrospective**
   - The next day's retrospective centers on learning rather than blame. The team reflects on:
     - What went well: Swift resolution through effective Swarming
     - What didn't go well: Missed testing and communication gaps
     - What they'll do next time: New testing protocols and regression tests for migration scripts
   - Tess admits her mistake, surprising Ravi and marking a turning point in team trust and dynamics.

4. **Team Growth**
   - Tess's vulnerability inspires openness, reducing blame and fostering trust.
   - The team celebrates their rapid recovery, reinforcing their collective resilience and commitment to improvement.

Key Concepts

1. **Retrospectives as Catalysts for Growth**
   - Retrospectives provide a structured framework for turning failures into actionable improvements, enabling teams to evolve continuously.

2. **Trust Through Vulnerability**
   - Openly acknowledging mistakes fosters a culture of trust and psychological safety, creating the foundation for honest collaboration and shared accountability.

3. **Recovering Through Collaboration**
   - Unified problem-solving during high-pressure moments reinforces adaptability, demonstrating how collective efforts transform setbacks into learning opportunities.

Themes and Takeaways

- **Learning Through Reflection**
  Retrospectives empower teams to address mistakes con-structively, fostering growth, adaptability, and continuous improvement.
- **Building Trust Through Vulnerability**
  Acknowledging mistakes without blame reduces conflict, strengthens cohesion, and establishes a culture of psycholog-ical safety.
- **Resilience Through Collaboration**
  Unified and swift problem-solving demonstrates the power of teamwork in navigating challenges and achieving success.
- **From Blame to Growth**
  Shifting the focus from assigning fault to learning and im-provement reinforces a growth mindset and drives transfor-mational change.

Conclusion

Chapter 7 captures a pivotal moment in Team Swaggernauts' journey, turning a major failure into an opportunity for growth. Through retrospectives and shared accountability, the team strengthens trust, fosters learning, and reinforces their commit-ment to resilience and collaboration.

Reflection Questions

- How do you approach failure within your team, and what changes could you make to turn setbacks into learning opportunities?
- What role do you play in creating a culture where team members feel safe to take risks and share mistakes?

Chapter 8

Commitment Revisited: Choosing Their Fate

The Aftermath of the Retro

After the retrospective, as Sprint Five kicked off, Team Swagger-nauts felt different. It wasn't something you'd spot on a dashboard or dissect in a sprint report. It was more subtle—something you could feel in the room.

The way Tess leaned in during discussions, offering ideas instead of snark. The way Ravi, for once, let his sarcasm take a backseat to actual collaboration. The way Amina stopped glancing nervously at the clock, as if time would betray her progress.

The first time it happened, Alex nearly missed it.

Tess was debugging a payments error on the shared screen. Her fingers hovered over the keyboard, her hesitation palpable. A silence stretched, but then she surprised everyone—including herself.

"Hey, QA," Tess said, her tone steady but softer than usual. "You see anything weird here?"

Ravi blinked, looking up from his laptop. "You…want my input?"

"Yeah," Tess replied, eyes still fixed on the screen. "I'm not seeing it. You got fresh eyes. Take a look."

Ravi didn't fire back with his usual quip. No sideways jab. No sarcasm. He just leaned in, his focus sharp. "Scroll up," he said, his voice calm and deliberate.

Alex didn't say a word. She just watched—feeling, for the first time, like she'd seen a sky once heavy with thunder finally clear, revealing blue. *Trust.* It's starting.

The Decision

The Swaggernauts gathered in the team room. This wasn't a normal meeting. Everyone knew it.

The air was thick, the kind of energy that lingers when something *big* is about to happen.

Alex stood at the front of the room, marker in hand, the whiteboard behind them starkly blank. She let the moment stretch, scanning the team before speaking.

"It's time," Alex said, her voice carrying just enough weight to hold the team's attention.

A few glances darted across the room. Tess crossed her arms, Ravi tilted his chair back, and Amina sat up straighter, intrigued.

Alex smiled. "Don't worry—it's not mandatory. I'm just going to *offer* something. And then it's up to you to decide."

The tension lifted. Curiosity replaced skepticism.

"Over the last few sprints, you've been operating as Dynamic Fractals," Alex continued. "You've taken on shared commitments. You've swarmed stories, limited WIP, and focused on finishing together instead of working alone. And it's paying off. You're starting to feel it, aren't you?"

Tess nodded, almost reluctant to admit it. Amina, though, spoke up without hesitation. "Yeah, I do. It's...different. Better."

"Good," Alex said with a grin. "Because here's the thing—we've been experimenting with the F.I.T. Formula. Today, I'm suggesting we make it official."

She turned to the whiteboard and wrote in bold letters:

F.I.T. Formula
- **Dynamic Fractals**
- **WIP Limits**
- **Teaming**
- **Commitment Language**

"This isn't a mandate," Alex clarified, turning back to the team. "But I'm seeing results, and I think you are too. When you commit together as a fractal, when you limit your work in progress, when you collaborate intentionally, when you make micro-commitments through Commitment Language—you *finish*. You've proven that much already."

Ravi smirked faintly. "So, what's the catch?"

Alex laughed. "No catch. It's a choice. I'm asking you to decide: Do we stick with it and go all in? Make the formula officially part of how we work every day? Make it our norm?"

Silence followed as the team absorbed the question.

Tess glanced at Ravi, who raised his hands in mock surrender. "Hey, don't look at me. I'm not the one dragging my feet anymore."

Amina's voice broke through the quiet. "I say we do it. I like working this way. It's less stressful because I know someone always has my back."

Tess uncrossed her arms, letting out a slow breath. "She's right. It's working." She looked at Alex. "We're in."

Across the room, nods followed. Even Kira, framed in her small video window, smiled and said, "Let's make it official."

F.I.T. in Action

That afternoon, the Swaggernauts moved like a team with a purpose.

Tess, Ravi, and Amina huddled together, laptops open and screens glowing as they swarmed a story. Tess built the framework, Ravi paired with Amina to tackle edge cases, and the three of them synced every thirty minutes, adjusting as they went.

In Fractal B, Liam and Sofia pulled Mateo into a Pairing session to crack an elusive bug. Across the room, in Fractal C, Nia and Ethan debated a database change, checking in frequently with Harper to validate their tests.

The room buzzed with focus and flow.

By the end of the day, Alex didn't need to ask. She could see it.

Stories moved across the board like clockwork. Conversations were sharper, calmer, and more deliberate. No one was hoarding tasks, and no one was left behind.

The next day's Daily Scrum was a testament to their new rhythm.

Tess spoke first. "Our fractal committed to the cart issue yesterday, and we got it done. Today, we're pulling the refund logic story and Swarming to finish it."

Ravi added, "I'm pairing with Tess on the implementation. Amina's running integration tests alongside us."

Fractal by fractal, the updates followed—clear, focused, and aligned.

Alex stood at the back of the room, a quiet smile tugging at her lips. The Swaggernauts had made the choice to own the formula, and the difference was undeniable.

Fractals. Focus. Flow.

And they were just getting started.

Chapter 8 Summary

In Chapter 8, Alex officially presents the F.I.T. Formula to the team, framing it as an optional yet transformative approach. Empowered by trust and visible results from their earlier experiments, the Swaggernauts choose to adopt the formula and immediately reap the benefits. The team solidifies its transformation from a group of individuals into a unified team.

Key Developments

1. **The Formula Becomes a Choice**
   - After a while working in the new way, Alex offers the F.I.T. Formula as a team decision rather than a mandate, giving ownership of the change to the Swaggernauts.

- The team votes unanimously to adopt the formula, recognizing its positive impact on their productivity and cohesion.

2. **Collaboration in Action**
   - On the first day of fully embracing the formula, fractals swarm stories, pair on challenging tasks, and demonstrate visible progress during the Daily Scrum.
   - Tess seeking Ravi's input during a debugging session reflects the team's growing trust and collaborative spirit.

Key Concepts

1. **Empowered Change Through Choice**
   - Offering the formula as a choice empowers the team, fostering deeper psychological investment and ensuring the change is sustainable.
2. **Team Ownership in Action**
   - The team's decision to adopt the formula demonstrates their commitment to collaboration, reinforcing shared accountability and trust.
3. **Momentum Through Visible Progress**
   - Immediate results, like stories moving across the board and clear commitments, inspire confidence and drive long-term improvement.
4. **Flexibility in Techniques**
   - While the core principles remain fixed, the team decides when, where, and how to apply techniques like Mobbing, Swarming, or Pairing, ensuring the system adapts to their needs and remains effective.

Themes and Takeaways

1. **Trust Fuels Collaboration**
   - Acts of trust, such as reaching out for help, reflect evolving team dynamics, enabling faster problem-solving and deeper collaboration.
2. **Momentum from Visible Wins**
   - Tangible outcomes, like stories moving forward, energize the team, creating a cycle of confidence, motivation, and continuous success.
3. **Sustainable Transformation Starts Within**
   - Empowering teams to choose their path ensures transformation is meaningful, lasting, and aligned with their values.

Conclusion

Chapter 8 highlights that true transformation occurs when change is embraced by choice, not imposed. Through trust, shared accountability, and collaborative progress, the Swaggernauts find their stride, ready to face future challenges as a united team.

Reflection Questions

- What visible progress was evident during the most recent experiment within your team?
- What behavior changes could you make to strengthen your team's psychological safety?

Chapter 9

Momentum in Motion: Winning One Day at a Time

The Energy Builds

Alex noticed it the moment she walked into the team space the following morning. The quiet hum of clicking keyboards wasn't new. What was new was the energy. The pace. The intensity. The focus.

Fractal A—Tess, Ravi, and Amina—was already huddled together, deep in discussion over a story. Tess had her hands flying across her keyboard, like a jazz pianist in full swing. Ravi leaned forward, pointing at her screen as he muttered something under his breath. Amina nodded thoughtfully, jotting down notes on a sticky pad.

Fractal B—Liam, Sofia, and Mateo—wasn't far behind. Sofia and Liam had their laptops open, pairing on a critical feature, while Mateo worked on writing the integration tests alongside them. Their conversation flowed smoothly, with the occasional burst of laughter breaking the intensity.

Fractal C—Nia, Ethan, and Harper—was in the far corner, standing around the Kanban board. They gestured toward a sticky note in the "In Progress" column, debating how to split a story into smaller tasks.

Alex leaned against the wall, arms crossed, taking it all in.

They weren't working harder. They were working differently.

"Alright, everyone—Daily Scrum time!" Alex clapped her hands together. "Let's hear it. Fractal commitments only. What's your fractal committing to today?"

The Commitment Circle

Alex pulled out the whiteboard marker and wrote "Fractal Commitments" at the top of the board. "Fractal A, you're up first," Alex quipped.

Tess, Ravi, and Amina stepped forward together. Tess spoke for the group. "We're finishing the payment gateway exception handling logic, writing the error tests, and running regression tests to validate."

Alex raised an eyebrow. "That's ambitious. You think you'll finish all of that today?"

Tess nodded confidently. "We've already broken it into smaller chunks. Amina's handling unit tests. Ravi's prepping the edge cases for regression testing. I'll drive the main implementation."

Alex grinned, writing it down: "Fractal A: Payment gateway exception logic, error tests, regression validation."

"Fractal B, you're next," Alex prompted.

Sofia stepped forward. "We're tackling the subscription flow edge cases. Liam and I will pair on fixing the logic, and Mateo's handling the test automation for it."

Alex wrote: "Fractal B: Subscription flow edge cases, logic fixes, and test automation." Fractal C, your turn," Alex said, turning to Nia, Ethan, and Harper.

Nia took the lead. "We're splitting up the refund logic story. Ethan's addressing the database schema changes, Harper's testing the APIs, and I'm handling the business logic."

Alex nodded, writing: "Fractal C: Refund logic—schema updates, API testing, business logic."

"Alright, everyone," Alex said, capping the marker. "No solo heroes, no unfinished stories. If something blocks you, call for help. If you finish early, pull the next priority. Clear?"

There were no complaints. No groans. Just nods and focused eyes. They were in it now.

Small Wins, Big Momentum

At 10:22 a.m., Fractal A hit their first milestone. Tess leaned back, watching the unit tests pass. All green. No bugs. No failures.

"Amina, push the tests," Tess called.

Amina nodded, her fingers dancing across her keyboard.

Ravi glanced over. "Run it twice," he suggested. "Sometimes timing logic breaks on the second pass."

Tess frowned but followed his advice. The tests ran again. All green.

"Happy?" Tess asked, glancing at Ravi.

"Yeah. Happy," Ravi said with a faint grin.

At 1:14 p.m., Fractal B celebrated their own win. Liam stretched and leaned over to Mateo.

"Tests are clean," he said, tapping the table. "Subscription flow is airtight."

Sofia glanced up, surprised. "Already?"

Liam grinned. "Teamwork, Sofia. It works."

By 2:49 p.m., Fractal C's Slack channel lit up.

Nia: "Refund logic is complete. APIs are validated. Harper crushed it."

Alex: "Nice! Marking it DONE."

Celebrating the Wins

At the end of the day, the team gathered around the "Fractal Commitments" board. Alex circled the words "DONE" next to each fractal's name.

- Fractal A: Payment gateway exception logic, error tests, regression validation—DONE.
- Fractal B: Subscription flow edge cases, logic fixes, and test automation—DONE.
- Fractal C: Refund logic—schema updates, API testing, business logic—DONE.

Ravi leaned forward, hands on his hips, squinting at the board. "Wait, wait, wait. We all finished? All of us?"

Tess turned her head, squinting like it might be a trick. "Huh."

"Y'all better take a picture of that," Kira said from the conference screen, laughing. "That's history right there."

Alex pulled out her phone and snapped a quick picture of the board.

"This is what winning looks like," Alex said. "This is what done feels like."

Engagement Unlocked

On Friday, something unexpected happened.

Fractal A arrived twenty minutes early. Tess was already reviewing edge cases, Ravi was prepping a fresh set of tests, and Amina was sketching out diagrams for their next story.

"Alright, Fractal A," Alex called out at the Daily Scrum. "What's your commitment today?"

Tess didn't wait for Alex to prompt her further. "We're finishing the customer dispute logic today," she said, glancing at Ravi and Amina. "End of day, it's done."

Amina nodded, adding, "I'm running tests alongside implementation."

Alex grinned. "That's what I like to hear."

Chapter 9 Summary

Chapter 9 captures Team Swaggernauts fully embracing the F.I.T. Formula, leveraging fractal commitments to drive collaboration, accountability, and collective wins. By focusing on shared goals, the team begins to unlock a rhythm of sustainable success, transforming individual efforts into unified momentum.

Key Developments

1. **Fractal Commitments Drive Responsibility, Focus, and Accountability**
   - Fractals A, B, and C work collaboratively, setting clear daily goals and delivering on them as cohesive units.
   - Daily Scrums become opportunities for actionable commitments and alignment, minimizing silos.
2. **Shift in Team Dynamics**
   - Team members demonstrate increased accountability, arriving early and collaborating proactively to tackle blockers.
   - A cultural shift toward collective ownership and a "win together" mentality becomes more evident.
3. **Momentum from Small Wins**
   - The team continues to experience how incremental successes build confidence and energize future efforts, creating a positive feedback loop.
4. **Stronger Collaboration**
   - Fractals adapt dynamically, calling out blockers and offering support, showing how shared responsibility enhances delivery.

Key Concepts

1. **Fractal Commitments**
    *   Unified, actionable goals set during Daily Scrums ensure alignment, accountability, and coordination across the team, reducing silos.

2. **Shared Ownership in Action**
    *   By attributing success or failure to the entire fractal, the team fosters a culture of mutual responsibility, reducing finger-pointing and strengthening cohesion.

3. **Momentum Through Incremental Wins**
    *   Breaking work into manageable tasks and completing them as a unit creates a rhythm of progress that energizes the team and sustains motivation.

4. **Driving Results with the F.I.T. Formula**
    *   Dynamic Fractals, WIP Limits, Teaming, and Commitment Language work seamlessly together, enabling the team to overcome challenges and deliver results.

Themes and Takeaways

1. **Winning Through Collaboration**
    *   Mutual accountability and shared goals highlight the power of teamwork, emphasizing that success is a collective effort.

2. **The Energy of Incremental Wins**
    *   Celebrating daily achievements fuels a virtuous cycle of motivation, progress, and sustained momentum.

3. **Proactive Engagement as a Culture**
    *   Early arrivals, initiative-taking, and active contributions signal a cultural shift toward a high-performing, deeply invested team environment.

4. **Trust as a Catalyst for Growth**

- Open discussions of commitments and blockers build trust, enabling transparency, experimentation, and continuous improvement.

Conclusion

Chapter 9 highlights the Swaggernauts' transformation into a high-performing, unified team, building momentum through collaboration and shared accountability. By embracing the F.I.T. Formula, the team solidifies their cultural shift, proving that lasting change is achieved one small win at a time.

Reflection Questions

- How do you celebrate small wins, and how does this impact your team's motivation?
- What daily habits could you adopt to maintain momentum and focus in your team's work?

Chapter 10

Breaking Barriers:
Pride, Progress, and Accountability

When Fractals Falter

Sprint Six was starting. There were ten days left until the Project UXcellence demo, and it felt like the wheels were coming off.

The workflow board, once neatly flowing with fractal-level commitments, now looked like a traffic jam. Stories had been stagnating in "In Progress" for far too long. Three critical ones were marked "blocked" in bright red, sending a clear signal: something was very wrong.

Alex scanned the room.

Fractal A—Tess, Ravi, and Amina—was silent. Tess's face was glued to her monitor, her hands frozen over her keyboard as though typing might unleash an avalanche. Ravi fidgeted with a pen, spinning it idly as his eyes darted between his phone and laptop. Amina watched the activity but looked hesitant to step in.

Fractal B—Sofia, Liam, and Mateo—sat huddled at their desks, but the tension between them was palpable. Sofia's arms were crossed as she stared at Liam, who was typing but occasionally glancing at her nervously. Mateo, the QA, looked frustrated, glancing between Jira and his screen. They were blocked, too, on a database configuration issue.

Fractal C—Nia, Ethan, and Harper—was trying to stay productive, but the strain was visible. Ethan was muttering about misaligned version dependencies within the code while Harper rubbed her temples. Fractal C was blocked, completing the trifecta.

The room had the unmistakable charge of something about to erupt.

Alex stepped to the front of the room, clapping her hands to get everyone's attention. "Alright, Swaggernauts, listen up. We've got an accountability problem."

All eyes turned to Alex, some reluctantly. Tess sat back in her chair, crossing her arms, her eyes narrowing. "Here we go…"

Alex tapped the whiteboard, where the three "blocked" stories sat like glaring accusations. "These are the stories holding us back, and we've got to address them now.

"Fractal A, let's start with you. That's your story stuck in 'In Progress' for five days."

Tess's eyes flashed. "We're working on it," she said sharply.

"Are you?" Alex shot back. Her voice wasn't raised, but it carried weight. "Because it's been five days, and I haven't seen movement. You committed to finishing it Tuesday. It's Friday."

Tess's chair creaked as she leaned forward, her tone icy. "Careful, Alex. You're walking a thin line."

Alex didn't flinch. "Yeah, I am. But it's the right line."

The room went still. Everyone was watching. Even the fractals that weren't directly involved seemed to hold their breath.

"Here's the truth," Alex continued, locking eyes with Tess. "You're stuck. And instead of asking for help, you're pretending you're fine. And it's killing our flow. That's not how this team works. Not anymore."

Tess opened her mouth to reply, but Alex wasn't done. "You know why I know this? Because I've done it too. We all have. It's called pride. We think we can push through on our own, but guess what? That's not the system we've built here. If one fractal is stuck, the whole team feels it."

Silence. The words hung in the air, heavy and undeniable.

Kira's voice broke the stillness from the conference screen. "He's right, Tess. We should've mobbed it days ago."

Ravi tapped the table with two fingers, leaning forward. "I kept thinking, 'Why hasn't Tess called for help?' We're ready, Tess. All you had to do was ask."

"We would help, too," Nia responded.

Tess's jaw tightened. She glanced at the whiteboard, her fractal-mates, and finally Alex. Her face softened, bit by bit, the tension draining like a deflating balloon. "Alright," she said quietly. "Call the mob."

The Fractals Mob

At 11:30 a.m., the fractals mobilized.

Fractal A took the lead. Fractals B and C observed. Tess shared her screen with the Scrum team, walking them through the problem. "It's the subscription logic," she explained. "It's supposed to handle exceptions for invalid payment tokens, but something's breaking."

Harper leaned in. "Why is that 'try/catch' block so big? Break it down."

"It's supposed to catch all payment errors," Tess replied, frowning.

"Yeah, but which one's causing the crash?" Sofia asked, pointing at the stack trace on Tess's screen.

Tess froze. Her eyes widened. "It's the null pointer," she muttered. "The null check is outside the 'try/catch.'"

Ravi nodded. "Oof. That'll do it."

Tess fixed the logic, and Ravi ran regression tests to validate the fix while Amina updated the Jira ticket. Within an hour, the blocker was cleared.

Over the next two hours, fractals B and C followed suit, Mobbing each other's blockers, with Alex facilitating the collaboration and the other fractals observing. Fractal B fixed a database misconfiguration, and fractal C resolved the code dependency issue.

By 3 p.m., the workflow board was alive with movement again. Stories moved from "Blocked" to "In Progress" to "Done."

The Lesson

Later that afternoon, Alex gathered the team for a debrief.

"Alright," Alex began, looking at the fractals. "What happened today?"

"We let stuff sit too long," Liam admitted, glancing at his fractal-mates. "We should've called for help sooner."

Tess nodded, her arms uncrossed for once. "I messed up. I thought I could fix it on my own. That wasn't fair to my fractal—or the team."

Alex nodded. "And what fixed it?"

"The mob," Ravi said. "Getting everyone together. No blame; just solutions."

Alex leaned forward, her voice steady. "This is what makes us different. We don't hide problems. We face them, together. Fractals own their commitments. And when one fractal is stuck, the others help. That's how we win."

Tess cracked a small smile. "Alright, alright. I'll call the mob next time."

"You better," Ravi teased.

The room filled with quiet laughter—a welcome release after the day's tension. They weren't just a group of fractals anymore. They were a team.

Chapter 10 Summary

In Chapter 10, Team Swaggernauts faces a crucial turning point just ten days before the Project UXcellence demo. A persistent blocker in Fractal A reveals deeper issues around pride and accountability, pushing Alex to confront these challenges head-on. By fostering collaboration through cross-fractal Mobbing and encouraging vulnerability, Alex helps the team restore momentum and strengthen their cultural transformation.

Key Developments

1. **Blockers**
   - A five-day blocker stalls Fractal A's progress, exposing Tess's reluctance to ask for help and the broader impact of unaddressed blockers on team momentum.
   - Other fractals had blockers, too, but were not asking for help outside the fractal.

2. **Accountability Conversation**
   - Alex addresses Tess directly, initiating a conversation about the role of pride and the importance of seeking support for the team's success.

3. **Team-Wide Mobbing**
   - Alex organizes cross-fractal Mobbing sessions to tackle persistent blockers, showcasing the power of collaborative problem-solving across the team.

4. **Cultural Breakthrough**
   - Tess's willingness to admit she's stuck signals a cultural shift, as fractals embrace vulnerability and trust to overcome challenges together.

5. **Momentum Restored**
   - All blockers are cleared, and the team regains focus and alignment, setting the stage for their upcoming demo.

Key Concepts

1. **Fractal Responsibility**
   - Fractals collaborate to resolve blockers as a unified team, breaking down silos and fostering shared responsibility for progress.

2. **Team-Wide Mobbing**
   - Mobbing extends across fractals, becoming a team-wide practice that maintains momentum and ensures critical blockers are resolved efficiently.

3. **Pride as a Barrier**
   - Pride emerges as an obstacle to collaboration, with the team learning that humility and openness are essential for sustained progress.

4. **Adaptive Leadership**
   - Alex's direct approach to addressing conflicts empowers the team to find solutions, reinforcing trust and enabling collaborative problem-solving.

Themes and Takeaways

- **Collective Ownership**
  - The team's ability to share responsibility and resolve blockers collaboratively strengthens cohesion and ensures steady progress.

- **Fostering Psychological Safety**
  - Tess's admission of being stuck reflects growing psychological safety, where openness enables deeper collaboration and trust.

- **Empowering Leadership**
  - Alex's leadership balances direct intervention with empowering the team, fostering autonomy while guiding problem-solving.

- **Breaking Pride to Build Progress**
  - Overcoming pride and fostering humility are pivotal steps toward achieving collective progress and sustaining team momentum.

Conclusion

Chapter 10 highlights the Swaggernauts' resilience as they confront pride and accountability head-on. By adopting cross-fractal Mobbing as a practice and fostering trust, the team clears blockers and regains momentum. Tess's personal growth mirrors the team's broader transformation, paving the way for a strong finish toward the Project UXcellence demo.

Reflection Questions

- How do you currently foster collective problem-solving behaviors within your team?
- What steps can you take to build stronger trust and collaboration when challenges arise?

Chapter 11:

The Final Push:
A Race Against Failure

The Unfolding Crisis

It was supposed to be a smooth day.

With only five days left until the demo, Team Swaggernauts was ahead of schedule. Six of the remaining eight critical features were marked "DONE," and the final two were in progress. For the first time, it felt like they might beat the deadline without breaking a sweat.

But crises don't wait for convenience.

Ravi froze mid-typing as he reviewed logs for his current task. "Tess," he called out, his voice sharper than usual.

Tess removed her headphones and glanced over, her eyes narrowing at Ravi's expression. "What?"

"Line 42 in the subscription logic," Ravi said, spinning his laptop around.

Tess leaned over, her brows furrowing as she read the code. Her eyes darted back and forth before she paled visibly.

"Oh no," she muttered. "No, no, no... That check is outside the conditional block. That's why it's passing invalid subscriptions."

"And it's live," Ravi added grimly.

Tess checked the deployment logs. Her breath caught. "Five days. It's been live for five days."

Across the room, Alex's head snapped up. "What's going on?" she asked, already walking over.

"The subscription logic," Tess explained, pointing at the screen. "It's a logic flaw. We've been granting expired users active access. For five days."

Alex's jaw tightened. This wasn't just a technical error—it was a potential catastrophe.

The Panic

Kira's voice blared from the conference screen, her face inches from the camera.

"What do you mean, five days?"

"Five days, Kira," Tess said, louder now. "It's been in production for five days."

Ravi sat up, his chair squeaking as he leaned forward. "You know what this means, right?" He glanced around the room. "It means every expired customer subscription for the past five days was marked as 'active.'"

"So, they got free access," Kira muttered, rubbing her temples.

"Yeah," Ravi said, arms crossed. "Not just free access. Some of them got premium features they didn't pay for."

The weight of it dropped on the room like a brick through a glass table.

Decisive Action

"Alright, listen up," Alex said, voice louder now, more commanding. She stepped to the front of the room. "We don't have time to panic. Here's what we're going to do."

She scanned the faces in front of them—Tess, Ravi, Amina, Kira on the screen, two other fractals nearby, all of them waiting for direction.

"We fix it. We repair the subscription validation bug. We get everything back to normal." Alex's eyes narrowed, voice sharp. "But we do it together. No solo work. No heroes."

"We swarm it."

"As fractals."

Tess nodded, rolling up her sleeves. "I'm in."

"This isn't about who caused it," Alex said, stepping toward Tess. "It's about who's going to fix it."

Tess looked up at Alex, her eyes softening. She nodded. "Yeah, I hear you."

"Then let's move."

The Fractal Swarm: Coordinated Action

Alex stepped up to the whiteboard, breaking the problem into three parallel tracks:

- Fractal A (Tess, Ravi, Amina): Refactor the broken validation logic and test fixes thoroughly.
- Fractal B (Liam, Sofia, Mateo): Audit and correct impacted customer data in the system.
- Fractal C (Nia, Ethan, Harper): Prepare the deployment and ensure smooth rollout of the fixes.

"This is full-team, cross-fractal Swarming," Alex declared. "Each fractal has its lane. If something blocks you, raise it immediately. If you finish early, pivot to assist another fractal."

"This is about collective ownership," Alex continued. "We swarm, we solve, we win."

Fractals in Action

The room buzzed with coordinated energy as each fractal dove into its tasks.

Fractal A: Fixing the Validation

Tess led the charge, refactoring the flawed logic.

"I'm moving the null check inside the conditional block," Tess said as her fingers flew over the keyboard.

"Good," Ravi replied. "I'll test edge cases as soon as you push."

Amina chimed in, "I'm adding regression tests for both active and expired subscriptions. We're not letting this happen again."

As Ravi ran initial tests, he flagged a subtle issue with premium subscriptions. "Tess, we need a separate condition for premium tiers."

"On it," Tess replied, her focus unshaken.

Fractal B: Correcting Customer Data

Across the room, Fractal B was deep into the database.

"Sofia, how many affected subscriptions do we have?" Liam asked.

"About three thousand two hundred," Sofia replied, scrolling through the results of her query.

Mateo added, "I'm verifying timestamps and matching them against the deployment logs. We can't miss edge cases."

"Once confirmed, I'll write a script to revert affected records," Liam said. "We'll need to cross-check it with the other fractals before we run anything."

Fractal C: Ensuring a Smooth Deployment

Fractal C was busy handling the logistics of the rollout.

"Harper, what's the status of the deployment pipeline?" Ethan asked.

"Staging is ready," Harper replied. "I'll queue up production after Fractal A pushes their changes."

Nia updated the documentation for stakeholders, ensuring they had clear communication about the fix.

The Fix

It took three hours.

Tess pushed her final changes. "Code is ready," she announced.

Ravi ran his last round of tests. "All green," he confirmed.

"Regression suite passed," Amina added. "No failures."

Sofia and Mateo flagged the data correction script as ready. Liam had the other fractals review it for approval, which was granted within minutes.

Harper's deployment pipeline showed no conflicts.

At 2:21 p.m., Harper clicked "deploy" on the pipeline. Everyone watched the status bar inch forward. When it hit 100%, the whole room let out a breath they didn't know they were holding.

Tess sat back in her chair, eyes closed, chest rising and falling like she'd just crossed a finish line. "Done."

"Done," Ravi echoed, grinning.

Alex stood before the team as relief swept through the room. "This is what Swarming is all about. Collective ownership. Multiple lanes. One mission. Well done, everyone."

The Ownership Moment

Later that day, Alex called a team meeting. Everyone gathered around the conference table.

"Alright," Alex said, eyes scanning the room. "What happened today?"

"I messed up," Tess said, not looking away this time. Her arms weren't crossed. "I wrote bad logic. I didn't see it. But I see it now."

Ravi tapped the table. "I missed it too. I tested it, but I didn't catch it."

116

Alex nodded. "And who fixed it?"

"We did," Tess said, nodding. She glanced around the room. "All of us."

Alex leaned forward, eyes sharp. "That's collective ownership." She tapped the table with one finger. "We win as a team. We fail as a team. We don't point fingers. We just fix it. Fast."

"Win together, fail together," Kira said from the conference screen, smiling.

Tess glanced at Ravi. For once, there was no sarcasm. Just respect.

"Yeah," Tess muttered. "Win together, fail together."

Chapter 11 Summary

Chapter 11 highlights the power of Swarming as Team Swaggernauts confronts a critical issue just days before the Project UXcellence demo. Their ability to handle parallel efforts and resolve the problem efficiently demonstrates their transformation into a high-performing team.

Key Developments

1. **The Crisis**
   - A subscription validation flaw, active for five days, inadvertently grants expired users access to the platform.
   - The team divides the problem into three parallel streams, tackling root cause analysis, code fixes, and deployment simultaneously.
   - Within three hours of focused collaboration, the fix is deployed with zero follow-up issues.

2. **The Ownership Moment**
   - Tess acknowledges her mistake in the flawed logic, and Ravi admits his testing oversight, demonstrating accountability and vulnerability.

- Alex reframes the experience as proof of the team's growth, emphasizing their shared mantra: "We win as a team. We fail as a team."

Key Concepts

1. **Cross-Fractal Swarming in Action**
   - The team leverages cross-fractal Swarming to collaboratively manage parallel efforts, demonstrating agility and focus during high-stakes challenges.
   - Each fractal owns their role within the swarm, reinforcing trust, cohesion, and shared accountability.

Themes and Takeaways

- **Adaptability Through Collaboration**
  - By drawing on the F.I.T. Formula, the team adapts to high-pressure situations, turning complex challenges into successful outcomes through real-time collaboration.
- **Structure as a Strength**
  - Dynamic Fractals and Teaming prove their value in navigating complexity, showing how structured approaches enable success under tight deadlines.
- **Accountability Drives Trust**
  - Openly owning mistakes and taking collective responsibility builds psychological safety and fosters continuous team growth.

Conclusion

Chapter 11 underscores the Swaggernauts' readiness for the Project UXcellence demo as they convert a crisis into a success story. Their seamless teamwork, accountability, and adaptability reveal a team fully prepared to meet challenges head-on.

Reflection Questions

- How do you own your mistakes, and how does this impact your team's alignment and trust?
- What behavior could you change to model the ownership you want to see from your team?

Chapter 12

Adapt, Align, Deliver Quickly: Tess Takes the Helm

The Calm Before the Chaos

Four days to the Project UXcellence demo.

The team space was peaceful. Quiet. Not "unproductive" quiet. The good kind of quiet. The kind of quiet where keyboards clacked in harmony and eyes stayed laser-focused on screens. There was no banter, no frivolous small talk—just the steady rhythm of real-time collaboration, low-volume verbal coordination, seamless task synchronization, and work being finished.

Alex walked slowly around the perimeter of the room, scanning the workflow board. It looked clean. Cleaner than it had in weeks.

- "Done" column: seven of eight critical features complete.
- "In Progress" column: one story—the final story. This would complete the last feature.
- "Blocked" column: Empty.

Alex stopped in front of the board, staring at it like it was a masterpiece in a museum. She'd never seen it this clean.

"You okay, boss?" Tess's voice broke the silence. She leaned back in her chair, eyes on Alex. "You look like you just saw a unicorn."

"Just admiring the work," Alex replied, tapping the "Done" column. "It's good. It's really good."

"Yeah, well, don't jinx it," Ravi called from across the room, tapping a bug log on his screen. "The sprint isn't over yet."

Tess chuckled. "He's not wrong, Alex. You know the second you celebrate, something's gonna break."

Alex smiled, shaking her head. "Not this time."

The Curveball

At 11:47 a.m., the email came in.

Kira's face appeared on the conference screen five minutes later, and it was clear she'd been on back-to-back calls. Her hair was disheveled, her eyes piercing with frustration.

"We've got a problem," Kira announced.

"Oh, come on," Tess groaned, spinning her chair in frustration. "I knew it. I knew it."

"This isn't my fault, Tess," Kira said, her tone sharp. She leaned forward toward the camera. "It's Nathan. He wants us to demo an entirely new story during the presentation. 'Subscription Upgrades.'"

The room went silent.

Alex felt her breath stop for a moment. Subscription Upgrades. It wasn't just a new story. It was a whole new feature.

"He wants it live?" Alex asked slowly, already knowing the answer.

"Yes, live," Kira replied, eyes tired. "He promised the board they'd see it on demo day."

Tess sat up straighter, her lips tightening, but this time there was no complaint. Instead, her brow furrowed in thought. She leaned forward, her voice confident. "Alright, then let's figure it out."

Alex quickly spun her head around, surprised but impressed. "Tess, go for it."

Tess Takes the Lead

Tess stood, walking toward the whiteboard. She grabbed the marker, writing the two bold words: "Subscription upgrades."

"Here's the breakdown," she began, her tone steady and deliberate. "It's three vertical slices. Each fractal will deliver an end-to-end piece of the feature."

She turned back to the team, meeting their eyes one by one as she continued. "We're not slicing by UI, back-end, or data integration. Each fractal owns an entire workflow—UI, business logic, and data updates. That way, we quickly deliver usable, testable value."

Tess drew three vertical columns on the board, writing under each:

- Fractal A: Upgrade from Free to Basic Plan
- Fractal B: Upgrade from Basic to Premium Plan
- Fractal C: Downgrade from Premium to Basic and Basic to Free Plans

She capped the marker, her gaze sharp. "Fractals A, B, and C, you each own your slice. You start from wireframe to deployment. No handoffs. You validate, integrate, and test your end-to-end flow."

Ravi raised his hand. "What if one fractal finishes early?"

"Then you support another fractal," Tess replied without hesitation. "We're all aiming for one thing: complete the feature by tomorrow. We sync every forty-five minutes. No blockers get ignored."

Alex smiled from the back of the room, her arms crossed. Tess had this.

Fractals in Vertical Motion

The team burst into action as Tess returned to her chair, pulling up the approved wireframes. She called out, "Ravi, Amina, use the wireframes from the previous sprint for the upgrade buttons. No deviations unless absolutely necessary."

"Got it," Ravi replied, opening the shared folder. "We're good here."

The fractals quickly divided tasks:

- Fractal A (Tess, Ravi, Amina): Owning the Free-to-Basic upgrade path, they designed the user flow, updated business logic, and validated the data changes.
- Fractal B (Liam, Sofia, Mateo): Focused on Basic-to-Premium upgrades, ensuring proper pricing validation and feature access changes.
- Fractal C (Nia, Ethan, Harper): Took on Premium-to-Basic and Basic-to-Free downgrades, managing the flow for removing premium features and adjusting subscription terms.

Real-Time Coordination

Forty minutes in, Fractal C hit a blocker. Nia called to Tess. "Tess, our downgrade flow is throwing a null pointer. Are you seeing similar issues in upgrades?"

Tess spun her chair to face her. "We had one earlier. It was in the token verification step. Check your conditional blocks for an edge case on expired tokens."

Ethan chimed in, "Got it. Testing now."

Five minutes later, Ethan called back, "Resolved! Thanks, Tess."

"Good work. Sync your logs with Ravi's script so we're consistent," Tess replied.

The Resolution

By 3:30 p.m., the fractals gathered for their final sync.

"Fractal A?" Tess asked, standing at the front.

"Free-to-Basic is done," Ravi announced. "Tests are green, and Sofia validated all database updates."

"Fractal B?"

"Basic-to-Premium is good to go," Liam replied. "We flagged one pricing bug, but it's resolved."

"Fractal C?"

123

"Premium-to-Basic and Basic-to-Free are solid," Nia said, smiling. "All downgrades reflect correctly in the API."

Tess nodded, turning to Alex. "We're ready for deployment."

"Tess, you're leading this," Alex replied.

Tess stood up. "Harper, kick off the pipeline. Once it's green, Ravi and Mateo will run final tests. If all's clear, we push to production."

Sigh of Relief

By 4:02 p.m., the "Subscription Upgrades" feature was live, and the team exhaled a collective sigh of relief. The room buzzed with a quiet pride as they reviewed their workflow board—clean, complete, and ready.

Kira's face appeared on the conference screen. Her usually tired eyes looked bright, and a rare smile spread across her face. "Team, I just got off a call with Nathan. He's thrilled. He doesn't know how you did it, but I do. This was nothing short of a miracle. Thank you."

The team exchanged glances, subtle nods of acknowledgment passing between them. Tess, still seated at the board, adjusted the marker in her hand, but didn't say anything.

Alex stepped forward, looking directly at Tess. "Before we wrap, I want to call something out. Tess, you didn't just help lead this—you owned it. You set the direction, kept us aligned, and drove this to success. That's what leadership looks like."

Tess blinked, caught off guard, and for a moment, her usual sarcasm disappeared. "I just… I just didn't want us to lose momentum," she said, shrugging as if to downplay her contribution.

Alex smiled. "Well, you didn't. You raised the bar for all of us today."

Kira chimed in. "Tess, they're right. You've always been brilliant technically, but this—this was something else. Thank you."

The room was quiet for a beat before Ravi broke the silence. "Alright, alright, let's not give Tess a bigger head than she already has."

Laughter rippled through the room, and even Tess smirked, rolling her eyes. "Thanks, QA."

As the team began packing up for the day, Alex lingered at the board, watching Tess update the workflow with the final task marked "DONE." For once, Tess didn't rush off. She stayed, leaning back in her chair, a rare look of satisfaction on her face.

It wasn't just another feature. It was proof of how far they'd come—together.

Chapter 12 Summary

In Chapter 12, the team faces a high-pressure insertion with only four days left. Tess steps into a leadership role, demonstrating confidence and decisiveness as she organizes the fractals to deliver vertical slices of value for the new "Subscription Upgrades" feature.

Key Developments

- **Tess Leads:** Tess confidently directs the fractals, ensuring tasks are divided into end-to-end deliverables.
- **Vertical Slicing:** Each fractal owns a full workflow, minimizing dependencies and maximizing delivery speed.
- **Real-Time Coordination:** Teams sync every forty-five minutes, but real-time problem-solving avoids unnecessary delays.

Key Concepts

- **Confidence Through Systems**
  - Tess's confidence, bolstered by the F.I.T. Formula and the team's shared system, enables her to step into a leadership

role during a defining moment, strengthening team trust and cohesion.

- **Real-Time Collaboration**
  - Fractals leverage real-time communication and shared responsibility to build the new feature, showcasing agile responsiveness and team alignment.
- **Vertical Slicing**
  - Delivering fully functional increments through vertical slicing maximizes value, minimizes integration risks, and ensures continuous progress.

Themes and Takeaways

- **Strength in Systems**
  - Tess's leadership moment highlights how reliance on well-designed systems creates poise, enabling individuals and teams to perform under pressure.
- **Agility Under Pressure**
  - The F.I.T. Formula demonstrates how Agile principles, like real-time collaboration and vertical slicing, enable teams to navigate complexity and deliver value, even in high-stakes situations.
- **Rising to the Challenge**
  - The team's cohesion and shared accountability transform a specification oversight into a milestone achievement, reinforcing the power of collective success.

Conclusion

Chapter 12 captures Team Swaggernauts raising the bar, with Tess stepping into her role as a leader and the fractals working in perfect harmony. Their ability to adapt to last-minute changes and deliver under pressure showcases their transformation into a high-performing team.

Reflection Questions

- How do you model resilience for your team during moments of high pressure or uncertainty?
- What is one thing that would better equip your team to adapt to unexpected challenges?

Chapter 13

The Final Demo: Thriving Under Pressure

The Big Day

The lights were harsh and cold, buzzing slightly in the Agilion Technologies conference hall. It was 9:57 a.m., and Team Swaggernauts was gathered at the front of the room. Over sixty executives and stakeholders filled the space, with another thirty attending virtually.

Nathan Cross, the CEO, sat in the middle of the front row. His expression was unreadable, his hands folded neatly in his lap. For a team that had spent six intense sprints transforming their workflow and delivery process, this was the moment of truth: the live demo of Project UXcellence.

Kira, as the Product Owner, stood in front of the presentation. She looked calm but alert, projecting the confidence she knew the team needed. To her side, the entire team sat at a long table, divided into their fractals but unified in purpose:

- Fractal A: Tess, Ravi, and Amina, to present Subscription Management.
- Fractal B: Liam, Sofia, and Mateo, to present Payment Integration.
- Fractal C: Nia, Ethan, and Harper, to present Error Handling and Resiliency.

Alex, the Scrum Master, stood at the side of the stage, watching intently, ready to jump in if needed. Alex had taken a deliberate step back to let Kira and the team shine.

Kira took a deep breath, scanning the room. "Good morning, everyone. Thank you for joining us today. On behalf of the team, I'm proud to introduce Project UXcellence—the next evolution of our subscription and payment platform." Her voice was steady, her words deliberate. This was Swaggernaut's moment.

The Setup

Kira clicked to the first slide, a sleek dashboard showcasing three main tabs: Payments, Subscriptions, and Account Management.

"The purpose of UXcellence is simple," Kira said, moving across the stage with practiced ease. "To create a seamless, unified experience for our customers. No more switching between tools or losing track of payments and subscriptions. Everything is in one place."

The next slide transitioned smoothly, displaying the key features of UXcellence:

- Subscription Management: Upgrade, downgrade, or cancel subscriptions with a single click.
- Integrated Payment Processing: A unified view of customer payments and invoices.
- Error Handling and Resiliency: Automatic retries and recovery for failed payments.

"These aren't just features," Kira continued, glancing back at the team. "They're the result of six sprints of collaboration, ownership, and relentless focus."

Behind her, Tess gave a subtle nod to Ravi, while Nia adjusted her notebook. They were ready.

"And now," Kira said, her smile widening, "we'll show you what this looks like in action."

The Walkthrough

Tess stepped forward first. The projector screen mirrored her laptop as she navigated to the Subscription Dashboard.

"This is the Subscription Dashboard," Tess explained, her voice clear and confident. "Here, customers can view their active subscriptions, upcoming renewals, and plan details—all in one place."

She clicked the Upgrade Plan button. A smooth animation transitioned the screen to the upgrade options. Tess smiled slightly, her confidence growing.

"With one click, customers can change their subscription tier," she said. "No waiting on support, no hidden fees. And every change is logged in real-time."

Ravi leaned forward from his seat. "And because we're obsessive about clean data, all changes are fully auditable." He glanced at Nathan. "No more guesswork."

Nathan's subtle nod was barely noticeable, but it was there.

Next, Liam took over, showcasing the Payments tab. "This is where customers can see all payment-related information at a glance," Liam said. He highlighted the invoice list, complete with real-time status updates.

"Failed payment? No problem," Liam added, transitioning to the error-handling screen. "The system automatically retries payments at optimal intervals, increasing success rates without manual intervention."

Finally, Harper stepped up, walking the audience through the Error Recovery Dashboard. "Every failed transaction is tracked and categorized," she said. "And when issues occur, the system sends automated alerts to support teams with clear resolution steps."

It was impeccable. The team flowed like a well-rehearsed orchestra, each section adding to the harmony.

The Glitch

Just as Harper finished, Tess transitioned back to the Payments tab for a final summary. She clicked once. Twice. Nothing happened.

The screen stayed frozen.

A sharp intake of breath rippled through the team. Alex's eyes darted to Tess, whose hand hovered over the mouse, her jaw tightening.

"Come on," Tess muttered, her voice low. She clicked again. Nothing.

Behind her, Ravi was already opening his laptop. "What's the issue?" he murmured, leaning toward Tess.

"API timeout," Tess said, her voice tight. "It's stuck on a 504."

"Swarm it," Alex mouthed quietly from the sidelines, nodding to the team.

Without hesitation, the fractals sprang into action. Harper researched the issue in the deployment logs, while Nia cross-checked the API calls against recent updates. Sofia joined Tess to inspect the request headers, looking for anomalies.

Ravi typed furiously. "Refreshing the API manually," he announced. "Give it five seconds."

"Try now," Sofia added, glancing at Tess.

Tess clicked the Payments tab again. The spinning wheel stopped. The page loaded instantly.

"Fixed," Tess said, her shoulders relaxing slightly.

"Boom," Ravi muttered with a grin, sitting back.

The Comeback

Kira stepped back in seamlessly, addressing the room with unwavering composure. "As you can see, the team and our system's resiliency shine even under pressure. And now, we'll continue."

The rest of the demo went flawlessly. Each fractal delivered their portion with precision and clarity. By the time Kira wrapped up with a final thank-you, the room was silent.

For three long seconds, nobody moved.

Then, Nathan Cross stood up. He clapped slowly, deliberately, before turning to the room. "This," he said, his voice calm but firm, "is what the future looks like."

Applause erupted, filling the conference hall. The team exchanged quiet smiles and nods. They had done it.

Aftermath

Back in the team room, the energy was charged with relief and pride.

"Alright," Alex said, standing at the center of the room. "What just happened out there?"

"We crushed it," Ravi said with a grin, leaning back in his chair.

"Yeah, the new platform is a huge success," Amina chimed in.

"Wow, we delivered all that in six sprints," offered Liam.

"And, even when things went sideways, we handled it," Tess added.

"And why?" Alex prompted.

"Because we trusted," Nia said, nodding toward the white board.

Alex smiled. "Exactly. You trusted each other, and you trusted the formula. That's what makes us a high-performing team."

Kira chimed in. "And for that, I'm incredibly grateful," she said, her expression warm. "The demo and the new platform were a massive success because of you—each of you. Thank you."

Alex turned to Tess. "And Tess, you set the tone. The way you led during that glitch. That was leadership."

Tess blinked, caught off guard. "I just…did what we had to do."

"And that's exactly why it worked," Alex said with a grin.

Tess smiled faintly, nodding. "Win together."

"Win together," the room echoed.

Chapter 13 Summary

Chapter 13 highlights the culmination of Team Swaggernauts' transformation as they tackle their biggest challenge yet: the live demo of Project UXcellence. Showcasing their teamwork, adaptability, and resilience under pressure, the team overcomes a mid-demo crisis to deliver a strong, confident presentation that wins over the audience.

Key Developments

The Stage
- Team Swaggernauts presents Project UXcellence to an audience of sixty executives, with an additional thirty attending virtually.
- Key features like subscription upgrades, integrated payments, and error-handling resiliency are showcased.

The Glitch
- During the Payments tab demo, the screen freezes, creating a critical moment of tension.
- Tess, Ravi, Nia, Harper, and Kira seamlessly transition into a swarm to troubleshoot the issue in real-time.

The Recovery
- Ravi quickly identifies a 504 API timeout as the issue and manually refreshes the request.
- Tess resumes the demo without hesitation, maintaining the team's composure and momentum.

The Verdict
- The presentation concludes successfully, receiving applause from the audience and an approving nod from Nathan Cross, the CEO.

Key Concepts

Composure Under Pressure

- The team exemplifies calmness and focus, leveraging their established Teaming practices to navigate the crisis with clarity and efficiency.

Swarming to Win

- Ad hoc Swarming showcases the power of shared accountability and collaborative expertise, enabling the team to resolve critical issues rapidly.

Confidence Through Recovery

- Successfully overcoming the glitch reinforces the team's resilience, building confidence in their ability to adapt and trust the F.I.T. Formula under pressure.

Themes and Takeaways

Trust in the System

- The team's confidence in the F.I.T. Formula and their established practices, such as Swarming and shared accountability, empowers them to make decisive, effective responses during crises.

Adaptability Over Perfection

- The team's composed response to unexpected challenges demonstrates that adaptability and teamwork are more impactful than striving for flawless execution, reinforcing their resilience and cohesion.

Collective Success

- The chapter underscores the power of teamwork, showing how a shared mindset of "winning together" creates a sustainable, high-performing culture.

Conclusion

Chapter 13 represents the triumphant climax of Team Swagger-nauts' journey. Their ability to deliver in six sprints and to adapt, collaborate, and recover under pressure not only validates their transformation into a high-performing team but also leaves them equipped to confidently face future challenges.

Reflection Questions

- What is currently done to intentionally create opportunities for skill-sharing and learning within your team?
- What behaviors could the team adopt to encourage deeper collaboration and collective growth?

Chapter 14

A New Standard: Rising Together

The Morning After

Once again, it was quiet. Peacefully quiet.

For the first time in weeks, there was no pressure hanging over the team. No ticking clock. No "X days to demo" written on the whiteboard in bold red ink. The countdown was gone. The pressure was gone. And for once, Team Swaggernauts wasn't moving at full sprint speed.

Tess walked in at 8:52 a.m., earlier than anyone else. No headphones this time. She sat down, took a deep breath, and looked around the room.

She leaned back in her chair, eyes drifting to the whiteboard. No "Blocked" column. No overdue tasks. No creeping sense of doom.

"Huh," she muttered, half-smiling to herself. "Feels weird."

At 9:10 a.m., Ravi showed up. Not his usual, slouched, "I just woke up" version, but alert, awake, on time. He walked in with a cup of coffee in one hand and a bag of mini-donuts in the other.

"Donuts?" Tess raised an eyebrow, clearly suspicious. "Since when do you bring donuts?"

"Since we won," Ravi replied, tossing the bag onto the table. He dropped into his chair, spinning once before facing Tess. "Team Swaggernauts eats like champions today."

Tess shook her head, grinning. "You're so dramatic."

"We earned it," Ravi said, leaning back, arms folded. "Can't argue with results."

The Email

At 9:23 a.m., Kira's face popped up on the conference screen. She was beaming, something Tess realized she hadn't seen in weeks.

"Y'all see the email?" Kira asked, eyes darting back and forth on her second monitor.

"What email?" Tess asked, taking a sip of coffee.

"Check it," Kira said, her grin growing wider. "Subject line: 'New Standard.' From Nathan."

Ravi's chair squeaked as he spun around, tapping away on his keyboard. "No way."

Tess opened her inbox. Sure enough, there it was. "New Standard"—from Nathan Cross.

She clicked it. Her eyes scanned the screen. Her face shifted slowly from curiosity to shock. She leaned forward. "No. Freaking. Way."

Subject: New Standard
From: Nathan Cross (CEO)
To: Company-Wide Distribution List

Team,

Yesterday, we witnessed something rare. We saw a team operate under pressure, face adversity, and adapt. More importantly, we saw them win—in six sprints—not because of luck, but because of structure, focus, collaboration, and accountability. Effective today, the F.I.T Formula used by Team Swaggernauts will be the new company standard for Agilion product development.

Dynamic Fractals. WIP Limits. Teaming. Commitment Language.

Team Swaggernauts has set the bar. Now, the rest of us will rise to meet it.

—Nathan Cross

Tess sat back, staring at the screen like it might change if she blinked too many times. "He just..." She glanced at Ravi, eyes wide. "He's copying us?"

"He called it 'the bar,'" Ravi said, leaning back with his arms folded. His grin was growing by the second. "We're the bar now."

Kira's voice chimed in from the screen. "Congrats, y'all. You just became the blueprint."

The Meeting with Nathan

At 11 a.m., Alex got called into a one-on-one meeting with Nathan Cross. It wasn't unusual to meet with Nathan, but this one felt different. There was no "bring the team" message. It was just Alex.

Nathan's office was sleek and minimalist. No clutter. No distractions. Just a large desk, a sleek leather chair, and a floor-to-ceiling window overlooking the city skyline.

Nathan didn't look up right away. He was typing something on his laptop, his fingers moving with precision. When he finished, he closed the lid, leaned back in his chair, and looked directly at Alex.

"Please, sit," Nathan said, gesturing to the chair across from him.

Alex sat.

"How do you feel?" Nathan asked.

Alex blinked. "About the demo?"

"About all of it," Nathan said, folding his hands together. "The demo. The team. Your role."

Alex took a moment, hands on her lap. "I feel...proud."

Nathan nodded slowly. "Good answer."

The silence between them lingered for a moment, but it wasn't awkward. It felt deliberate. Nathan was waiting.

"I'm going to tell you something important, Alex," Nathan finally said, leaning forward. "Leadership isn't about control. It's about trust. Trust that when you step back, the team steps forward."

Alex nodded, absorbing the words like they were being carved into stone.

"You did that," Nathan continued. "You built something bigger than you." He leaned back, tapping the desk lightly. "Most people think leadership is being in charge. It's not. It's letting go."

Alex felt something shift in her chest, like hearing something she'd always known but had never understood until now.

Nathan leaned forward again. "I've seen leaders rise. I've seen them fall. You're rising, Alex. And I want you to keep rising."

"Thank you, Nathan," Alex said, feeling the weight of those words settle on her shoulders. "I won't let you down."

"No," Nathan said, his eyes sharp. "Don't say that. Don't say you won't fail. Say you'll learn."

Alex nodded slowly. "I'll learn."

Nathan smiled. "Good."

The Transformation of the Team

Back in the team room, everything felt different. Not because of the email. Not because of Nathan. It felt different because they were different.

Tess no longer rolled her eyes when people called a swarm. She called them first.

Ravi didn't complain about edge cases anymore. He found them before they became problems.

Kira wasn't just "managing stakeholders"— she was a strategist, always thinking five moves ahead.

Alex didn't hover. She didn't micromanage. She didn't need to. She trusted.

And the rest of the team?

- Nia, once hesitant to voice her ideas, now led discussions on deployment strategies, ensuring pipelines were optimized for every sprint.

- Amina, initially focused solely on her tasks, had become the team's go-to for automating repeatable processes, sharing scripts and teaching others to streamline their work.
- Sofia, previously working quietly in the background, now actively drove collaboration between fractals, bridging communication gaps effortlessly.
- Mateo, often reserved and technical, had stepped up as the team's problem solver, tackling complex bugs and guiding newer team members through debugging sessions.
- Ethan, whose contributions had once been purely technical, now stepped into a mentoring role, helping junior developers and fostering a culture of growth.
- Harper, known for her perfectionism, had learned to balance quality with delivery speed, ensuring the team met deadlines without sacrificing standards.
- Liam, once focused only on coding tasks, had evolved into the team's architect, designing scalable solutions and ensuring technical alignment across fractals.

At the next sprint planning meeting, nobody argued over scope. Nobody fought over roles. They broke into fractals and teamed automatically. They maintained tight WIP Limits. They shared clear, specific commitments each day. They asked for help before things got stuck.

They didn't just know how to win now; they expected to win.

Closing the Loop

On Friday, as the week ended, Tess leaned back in her chair, arms folded.

"So, now that we're the bar, what do we do?" she asked.

Ravi shrugged. "Raise it."

Tess glanced at him, grinning. "Alright, QA. Let's raise it."

Chapter 14 Summary

Chapter 14 marks a milestone in Team Swaggernauts' journey, as their transformation into a high-performing team not only earns company-wide recognition but also sets a new standard for product development across the organization.

Key Developments

1. **Recognition as the New Standard**
   - The Swaggernauts' success with Project UXcellence positions them as a model team for others in the organization to emulate.
2. **Personal and Team Growth**
   - Individual growth is evident across all team members, showcasing how their collective transformation has fostered confidence and skills.
3. **Alex's Leadership Evolution**
   - Alex embraces a leadership style rooted in trust and empowerment, stepping back to allow the team to take full ownership of their success.

Key Concepts

1. **Leadership Through Trust**
   - Alex adapts her leadership style by empowering the team and trusting her ability to execute independently, avoiding micromanagement.
1. **Cultural Evolution**
   - The Swaggernauts demonstrate collaboration, accountability, and continuous improvement as second-nature behaviors, showing how cultural shifts are sustained through consistent practices.

1. **Raising the Bar**
   - The team adopts a growth mindset: rather than settling for being the standard, they commit to continually raising expectations through measurable goals and challenging themselves.

Themes and Takeaways

- Sustainable Transformation
  - The chapter underscores how meaningful change is built on trust, collaboration, and incremental progress.
- The Ripple Effect
  - The Swaggernauts' success inspires a cultural shift across the organization, highlighting the power of systemic change.
- Empowering Leadership
  - Alex's growth as a leader highlights the importance of empowering teams to thrive on their own while maintaining a shared vision and alignment.

Conclusion

Chapter 14 celebrates the Swaggernauts' evolution into a cohesive, high-performing team whose success resonates far beyond their individual achievements. Their transformation sets a new standard for excellence, reflecting the lasting impact of trust, collaboration, and continuous improvement.

Reflection Questions

- What current actions, behaviors, or systematic characteristics either foster or hinder raising the bar within your team?
- What new behaviors could leaders do to practice stepping back?

Chapter 15

The Ripple Effect: Scaling Success

The Request

It began as a Slack message from someone Alex barely knew.

[10:12 a.m.] Chris S. (Team Orion): "Hey Alex, got a second? Need some advice on fractals."

Alex squinted at the screen. Chris S. from Team Orion. They'd spoken a few times during company-wide sprint reviews, but never directly. Team Orion was known for being "the fast movers"—the team that prided itself on speed, even if it sometimes came at the cost of quality.

Alex replied.

[10:13 a.m.] Alex Morgan (Team Swaggernauts): "Sure thing. What's up?"

Ten minutes later, Alex was on a video call with Chris.

Chris had messy, curly hair and the kind of energy that felt like he was constantly moving, even when he wasn't. His eyes darted around the screen as if scanning for exits, but his voice was direct.

"So, I'm just going to say it," Chris said, leaning forward. "I think we're drowning."

Alex raised an eyebrow. "Drowning?"

"Yeah," Chris replied, rubbing his face with both hands. "We've got too many stories in progress. Like, eighteen at once. Everyone's touching everything, and nobody's owning anything. Every retro, it's the same conversation. 'Why didn't we finish more?' 'What's taking so long?' I'm over it."

Alex nodded slowly. "Sounds familiar."

"I heard you're doing something different," Chris said, pointing at the camera. "Dynamic Fractals or something?"

"Dynamic Fractals," Alex replied, sitting up straighter. "Small teams inside the team. A team of teams. Each fractal works only one story at a time. Three people are ideal; four people, max. No handoffs. Full ownership."

Chris tilted his head, thinking. "Three people?"

"Three," Alex repeated. "It's small on purpose. Small teams move faster."

Chris leaned back, his eyes shifting upward like he was running calculations in his head. He nodded slowly. "Alright. Tell me how to start."

"How many engineers do you have?" Alex asked.

"Seven," replied Chris.

"Okay, then you'll run two fractals. One fractal of three engineers and another fractal of four engineers," Alex advised. "It's best to let the engineers self-select but give them some ground rules to follow to maintain skill diversity. For example, no more than two senior developers and at least one test engineer in a single fractal," Alex added.

"Are those fixed?" Alex inquired.

"Glad you asked. No, they're not. They should be dynamic from sprint to sprint. The team is empowered to change their fractals each sprint. It's up to them, but the ground rules are followed. However, it may be easier to stay static at the beginning. Then, after they get the hang of it, move to switching," offered Alex.

The First Copycat

That week, Team Orion started running fractals.

Day 1 was chaos. People questioned it. One developer even said, "This is stupid. We're not Swaggernauts."

But by mid-sprint, something changed.

Chris pinged Alex again.

[3:43 p.m.] Chris S. (Team Orion): "This is wild. We're finishing faster. People are talking to each other. How did you get them to buy in so fast?"

[3:45 p.m.] Alex Morgan (Team Swaggernauts): "I didn't. They saw it working."

The Culture Shift

It wasn't just Team Orion.

Word spread. People talked. At company happy hours, Slack channels, and during sprint reviews, the phrase kept popping up:

"Have you seen how Swaggernauts works?"

People started asking questions.

- "What's this 'Teaming' thing they do?"
- "How do they finish stories so fast?"
- "What's a fractal?"

It wasn't long before other teams started copying it.

- Team Pegasus adopted WIP Limits and reduced their "In Progress" column from eleven stories to three while increasing flow.
- Team Eclipse began experimenting with Mobbing, calling for help at the first sign of a blocker. The number of blocked stories dropped dramatically.
- Team Orion became full converts to fractals, with Chris posting weekly wins in the company-wide Slack channel.

The Meeting with Nathan

At the next leadership sync with department leads and senior managers, Nathan called attention to it.

"I want to highlight something," Nathan said, tapping his pen on the conference table. "This company has spent years chasing 'best practices.' But in the past month, we didn't chase a practice. We followed a team."

He clicked on the screen behind him, revealing a slide with one word: "Swaggernauts."

"This team didn't just hit a deadline. They changed how we think. Now we have three other teams following their system. And from the reports I'm getting, they're seeing similar results."

Nathan glanced around the table, eyes sharp. "So, my question to all of you is this: Why aren't we all doing this?"

Silence.

No one had an answer.

Other Teams React

Not everyone was on board.

One manager, Derek from Team Polaris, raised his hand. "Look, I respect Swaggernauts, but this feels like a fad. Every year, it's something new. How do we know this isn't just the shiny new thing?"

Derek's pushback wasn't surprising. He came from a traditional leadership background, where command-and-control practices were the norm, and success was measured by how well he kept every detail in line. He thrived on micromanagement, often stepping in to make decisions for his team rather than empowering them to solve problems on their own. A firm believer in rigid hierarchies, Derek had built his career on ensuring processes were followed exactly as prescribed, often at the expense of innovation and team morale.

While his meticulous nature delivered short-term results, it also fostered a culture of dependency, where team members hesitated to take initiative or own their work. Deep down, Derek cared about the team's success but struggled to relinquish control, fearing that loosening his grip would lead to chaos.

Nathan's eyes shifted to Derek. "You think this is a fad?"

"I'm just saying," Derek shrugged, "not every team is Swaggernauts. They've got strong players. You can't just copy-paste strong players like that."

Nathan leaned forward. "That's the point, Derek. They don't just have 'strong players.' They have a strong system."

He tapped the table with his index finger. "They didn't win because Tess is a superstar or Ravi is a 10x engineer. They won because they built a system that makes everyone play better."

The room went quiet again.

Back at Team Swaggernauts

Back at the team space, Tess, Ravi, and Alex watched the recording of the leadership sync.

"Did he just…" Ravi leaned forward, eyes wide. "Did he just call us the system?"

Tess sat back, arms folded, grinning like she'd just won a bet. "He sure did, QA."

"We're famous," Ravi muttered, running a hand through his hair. "We're literally famous inside the company."

Alex didn't say anything for a while. She just watched the recording again, eyes examining Nathan's face.

"He's going to want more," Alex said quietly.

Tess rolled her head. "More?"

"More," Alex repeated. "He's going to want us to teach it. To scale it."

Tess sat forward, suddenly serious. "So, what do we do?"

Alex glanced at the whiteboard. "We raise the bar."

Scaling the System

Two weeks later, Nathan made the official announcement.

"We're launching the Swaggernauts Guidebook."

It wasn't just for Team Swaggernauts anymore. It was for everyone. The system was codified into the four components of the F.I.T. Formula:

- Dynamic Fractals
- WIP Limits
- Teaming
- Commitment Language

Each team was given a Swaggernauts Guidebook with principles, concepts, ground rules, and examples from Team Swaggernauts' journey. Every team member on Swaggernaughts was listed as contributors.

Training sessions began the following week.

The First Training

On the first day of training, Team Swaggernauts sat at the front of the room. In front of them were thirty-one people from Team Polaris, Team Eclipse, and Team Orion.

Alex stood at the front, arms crossed, eyes scanning the room.

"Good morning, everyone," Alex said, tapping the whiteboard. "This isn't theory. This isn't fluff. This is the formula we used to hit a deadline that we had no business hitting." She drew a large circle on the board. Inside it, four smaller circles. "This is the F.I.T. Formula," Alex said, underlining the words. "And by the end of this session, it's going to be yours too."

Chapter 15 Summary

Chapter 15 captures how Team Swaggernauts' innovative practices go beyond their team, sparking a company-wide transformation. What began as a bold experiment becomes the foundation for a new standard across the organization.

Key Developments

The First Inquiry

- Chris from Team Orion reaches out to Alex for advice on implementing fractals, marking the beginning of the Swaggernauts' influence on other teams.
- Despite initial chaos, Team Orion experiences faster results and improved collaboration after adopting the F.I.T. Formula.

The Cultural Shift

- Teams like Pegasus and Eclipse began to emulate Swaggernauts' practices, incrementally integrating elements into their workflows.
- Success stories shared via Slack and during reviews generate curiosity and momentum across the organization.

Leadership Recognition

- Nathan Cross highlights Team Swaggernauts' impact during a leadership sync, calling them the new standard for product development.
- Skepticism from a manager is countered by Nathan's emphasis on the systemic foundation of Swaggernauts' success.

Scaling the System

- Nathan announces the creation of the "Swaggernauts Guidebook," codifying their approach into a scalable, yet flexible framework.
- Alex leads training sessions to help other teams adopt the system.

Key Concepts

Cultural Transformation

- Team Swaggernauts inspires a company-wide shift, demonstrating how one team's transformation and success can influence an entire organization.

Systemic Thinking

- By leveraging the F.I.T. Formula, the Swaggernauts highlight the importance of designing scalable team structures that prioritize the strength of the system over individual talent.

Scaling Innovation

- Codifying their approach into the Swaggernauts Guidebook ensures that core principles, such as Dynamic Fractals, WIP Limits, Teaming practices, and Commitment Language remain intact. At the same time, the guidebook provides guidance on how other aspects can be adapted to meet the unique needs of different teams and contexts, ensuring scalability without compromising the integrity of the F.I.T. Formula.

Themes and Takeaways

Leadership Influence

- Alex transitions from a single team to becoming a transformational leader, influencing and inspiring change across the organization by fostering alignment, trust, and a shared vision for success.

Aligned Flexibility

- By adhering to fixed principles such as Fractal size, WIP Limits, Teaming practices, and Commitment Language, while allowing flexibility in how these principles are implemented within different contexts, the Swaggernauts strike a balance between alignment and adaptability. This ensures their approach remains scalable without compromising the integrity of the F.I.T. Formula.

System Over Talent

- Nathan's insight that Swaggernauts' strength lies in their system, not just their people, reinforces the importance of creating an environment that elevates everyone.

Conclusion

Chapter 15 illustrates how the Swaggernauts' journey evolves into a company-wide movement. Their practices inspire cultural transformation, serve as a replicable framework, and solidify their role as change-makers within the organization.

Reflection Questions

- How do you personally contribute to scaling your team's success beyond its immediate context?
- What behaviors do you need to model to inspire other teams or departments to adopt effective practices?

Chapter 16

Guiding the Shift: Teaching Through Experience

From Builders to Teachers

It felt different this time.

For months, Team Swaggernauts had been the ones doing the work, taking on deadlines, clearing blockers, and pushing each other to be better. They'd grown through the pressure, fought through the doubt, and come out stronger.

But this? This was different.

"I'm not a trainer," Tess muttered, arms crossed, leaning back in her chair.

Alex stood at the front of the room, marker in hand, tapping the whiteboard. "You're not a trainer, Tess. You're a leader."

"Sounds like the same thing," Tess muttered.

Alex glanced at her. "It's not." She tapped the board again. "A trainer gives you information. A leader gives you perspective."

Tess tilted her head, thinking. She didn't answer, but she also didn't argue.

The whiteboard had three big words at the top: "Swaggernauts Guidebook."

Below it was the four principles:

1. Dynamic Fractals
2. WIP Limits
3. Teaming
4. Commitment Language

"Here's the deal," Alex said, turning to the whole team. "We've been asked to build upon the initial training we gave. Now, we're going to provide hands-on workshops for Team Polaris, Team Eclipse, and Team Orion. Three teams. Three very different personalities. Training stuck in some teams and not so much in other teams."

"Team Orion is already on board," Kira said, her voice coming through the video screen. "Chris loves this stuff. He's already been copying us."

"Yeah," Tess said, leaning forward. "But Team Polaris? Forget it. Derek's been trash-talking this process for weeks."

"Doesn't matter," Alex said, arms crossed. "We don't convince them with words. We convince them with wins."

"How?" Ravi asked, his face skeptical.

Alex grinned. "Same way we convinced you."

"Oh, no," Tess said, squinting at Alex. "You're not doing that, are you?"

Alex's grin grew wider. "Oh, yes I am."

The First Workshop

At 9 a.m. on Monday, Team Polaris filed into the training room. There were eight engineers, not including their lead, Derek, who walked in with his arms crossed like he'd already decided this was a waste of time. Their Scrum Master and Product Owner also attended.

"Alright, let's get this over with," Derek said, dropping into his chair with a loud thud.

Tess raised an eyebrow, glancing at Alex. "Yeah, this'll be fun."

Alex ignored Derek, turning to the rest of the team. "Welcome. Today, you're not just here to learn. You're here to experience."

She drew a large circle on the board. Inside the circle, she drew four smaller circles, each labeled with one of the four components:

Dynamic Fractals
WIP Limits

Teaming

Commitment Language

"You've seen this before. This is the F.I.T. Formula," Alex said, tapping the board. "But I'm not going to explain it. We're going to live it. Right here. Right now."

The Simulation

"Here's the challenge," Alex announced, grabbing a stack of index cards. "You have twenty minutes to process ten customer orders. Each order has three parts: data entry, validation, and approval."

She split the eight engineers into two groups of four.

Group 1 would follow their current method—the "old way."

Group 2 would follow the Swaggernauts method—Dynamic Fractals, WIP Limits of one story at a time, and collective ownership.

Ravi stood at the front, grinning. "Alright, ready? Go."

The Chaos of the Old Way

Group 1 immediately fell into old habits.

One person grabbed four orders at once. Another person started working on the approval step before the validation step was done. Nobody talked to each other. They just worked—fast, but messy.

- "Who's got Order 3?"
- "I thought you had it."
- "No, I'm working on 5."
- "Why is 2 still in progress?"

By the time ten minutes had passed, they had seven incomplete orders on the table, and people were visibly frustrated. "This process is garbage," one of them muttered, glancing at Derek.

Derek rubbed his face with his hands. "Just finish it," he muttered.

The Swaggernauts Method

Meanwhile, Group 2—using the F.I.T. Formula—worked differently.

- They formed a fractal of four people.
- They pulled one order at a time, completing it before starting another.
- Tess acted as the facilitator, making sure they followed the system.

Tess leaned in. "Don't grab two orders. Just one. Trust me."

The first order was slow. They fumbled. They second-guessed. But once they finished the first, the second order was faster. By the time they hit order 4, they were flying.

"Alright, we got it. Next order!"

"Validation complete—who's on approval?"

"I got it. Move it."

With ten minutes left, Team 2 was done. All ten orders were complete.

The Moment of Clarity

Alex stepped forward. "Alright. Stop."

Both groups froze. Alex walked up to Group 1.

"How'd that feel?" Alex asked.

One of them shrugged. "Chaotic."

"Why?"

"Because no one knew who was working on what," they replied. "I kept grabbing stuff, but so was everyone else. Too much overlap."

Alex nodded, then turned to Group 2. "How about you?"

One person grinned. "It felt slow at first. But then it clicked. We just...started finishing stuff."

"Why?" Alex asked.

The person thought for a second. "We had one job at a time. It was simple. We knew what 'done' looked like."

Alex let that hang in the air. She turned to Derek. "What do you think, Derek?"

Derek leaned forward, arms still crossed, but his face was different now. His eyes were on the completed stack of orders from Group 2.

He glanced at Group 1's table, where half-finished orders sat in a messy pile. Then back at Group 2's clean, complete stack.

He didn't say anything at first.

Then, slowly, he nodded. "Alright," he muttered. "I'm listening."

Resistance to Acceptance

Over the next few weeks, Team Swaggernauts hosted more workshops for Team Polaris, Team Eclipse, and Team Orion.

At first, it was slow. People questioned everything. They called the concepts "buzzwords" and "overhyped." But after they ran the simulations and saw how much faster, clearer, and more efficient it was, something shifted.

- Team Polaris adopted WIP Limits within a week.
- Team Eclipse began using Swarming sessions every Wednesday.
- Team Orion fully adopted the F.I.T. Formula, sending Alex a Slack message with the words:

"I hate that you're right, but you're right."—Chris

Chapter 16 Summary

Chapter 16 marks Team Swaggernauts' evolution from practitioners to mentors, guiding other teams through workshops and experiential learning to adopt the F.I.T. Formula.

Key Developments

Transitioning to Teaching

- Team Swaggernauts is tasked with leading workshops for teams Polaris, Eclipse, and Orion.
- Tess initially resists teaching, feeling more comfortable as a doer, but Alex reframes her role as offering leadership and perspective.

The First Workshop

- During a workshop with Team Polaris, a simulation contrasts chaotic "old way" methods with the organized Swaggernauts system.
- The team quickly observes the effectiveness of the F.I.T. Formula in fostering ownership and efficiency.

Shifting Perspectives

- Derek, a skeptical lead from Team Polaris, changes his stance after witnessing the system's tangible results, becoming more open to adopting its principles.

Scaling Across Teams

- Over time, other teams adopt aspects of the Swaggernauts system:
  - Team Polaris implements WIP Limits.
  - Team Eclipse introduces Swarming one day a week.
  - Team Orion fully adopts the F.I.T. Formula, with Chris championing its success.

Key Concepts

Benefits Through Experience

- The Swaggernauts allow others to experience the benefits firsthand, using experiential learning to turn skepticism into advocacy.

Accelerating Buy-In

- Demonstrating small, tangible victories accelerates buy-in and drives systemic change.

Cultural Unification
- Broad adoption begins to unite teams under shared principles, fostering a cohesive organizational culture.

Themes and Takeaways

Lead With Results
- Alex and the team prioritize hands-on learning, letting results speak louder than words.

The Power of Tangibility
- True transformation takes time and patience, requiring others to tangibly experience the value of change.

From Resistance to Advocacy
- Clear, demonstrable benefits can turn skeptics into champions of change.

Conclusion

Chapter 16 demonstrates Team Swaggernauts' ability to inspire and lead organizational transformation. By running workshops and sharing their system through hands-on experiences, they enable other teams to replicate their success, fostering a unified, high-performing culture across the company.

Reflection Questions
- How do you balance teaching others with allowing them space to discover their own solutions?
- What behaviors can you adopt to make your coaching or mentoring more impactful?

Chapter 17

The Podcast:
An Invitation to Legacy

The Email That Changed Everything

It was a Tuesday morning when Alex received the email. Alex opened the message, eyes squinting at the screen.

Subject: "Podcast Invite—Lessons from Swaggernauts"
From: Rachel C., Host of The Agile Mindset Podcast

Hi Alex,

I've been following the story of Team Swaggernauts ever since your company's CEO, Nathan Cross, mentioned you in his LinkedIn post. It's clear your team is doing something special. I'd love to have you on The Agile Mindset Podcast to discuss how your team created and scaled the Swaggernauts Guidebook.

Our audience of Scrum Masters, Agile Coaches, and Team Leads would love to hear about your approach and how you built collective ownership.

Let me know if you're open to a forty-five-minute episode.

Best,

Rachel C.

Host, The Agile Mindset Podcast

Alex's eyes moved slowly from the email to the whiteboard at the front of the room, where today's Daily Scrum commitments were written.

Alex glanced at Tess.

"Hey, Tess."

Tess didn't look up. She was already knee-deep in her work. "What?"

"We're famous."

Tess stopped typing. Slowly, she turned in her chair, eyes narrowed in suspicion. "What did you do, Alex?"

"Nothing," Alex replied, arms crossed, still looking at the screen. "But apparently, Nathan wrote about us on LinkedIn."

"Oh, no," Tess muttered, pulling off her headphones. "Please tell me he didn't say 'world-class' again."

Alex scrolled to find the post. It was worse.

Nathan Cross—CEO at Agilion Technologies

"When people ask me what 'excellence' looks like, I tell them about Team Swaggernauts. This team didn't just deliver a project. They created a new way to work—a system that scales. A system that works.

The Swaggernauts Guidebook is now our standard, but it won't stay ours for long. Other companies will notice. Other teams will copy it.

That's fine with me. Because if the world gets better because of Team Swaggernauts, that's a legacy worth building."

Ravi whistled, eyes wide. "Legacy, huh?"

Tess raised her head back, groaning. "We're gonna have to do interviews, aren't we?"

"Not if I ignore this email," Alex muttered, hovering over the "Archive" button.

"Don't do that," Tess said, eyes narrowing. "Don't be that person, Alex."

Alex smiled. "You're right. We need to do this."

The Podcast

One week later, Alex sat in front of a microphone in a small recording room, headphones on. The red recording light glowed steadily.

"Welcome to The Agile Mindset Podcast." Rachel's voice echoed warmly in their headphones. "Today, we're talking to Alex Morgan, Scrum Master of the now-famous Team Swaggernauts. Their system for Dynamic Fractals, WIP Limits, Teaming, and Commitment Language has started to make waves in the Agile world."

Alex glanced at the camera, feeling the weight of it. *Here we go.*

"Welcome to the show, Alex," Rachel said. "Let's start with the obvious question. How did this all begin?"

Alex leaned forward. "It began with failure. That's the truth," Alex said, eyes focused on the camera. "We weren't some high-performing, magical team. We were just like every other team—too many stories in progress, blockers piling up, stories carrying over, and people feeling frustrated. The only thing we did differently was admit it. We admitted it wasn't working. And that's when things started to change."

The World Notices

After the podcast aired, the DMs started.

[12:43 p.m.] Sam (Agile Coach, LeanFlow Consulting): "Hey Alex, I heard you on The Agile Mindset Podcast. Amazing story. Any chance

I can pick your brain about Dynamic Fractals?"

[2:12 p.m.] Natalie B. (Scrum Master, Innovare, Inc.): "Alex! Just finished your podcast. Quick question: How do you handle fractal conflicts when two people have strong opinions on how to complete a story?"

[4:07 p.m.] Jeremy R. (VP of Product, FastLaunch Co.): "Alex, big fan of your work with Team Swaggernauts. We're trying to introduce Swarming at our company, but it's hitting resistance. Any advice on how to get buy-in from stubborn developers?"

Alex didn't answer all of them. But some, yes.

The next week, Kira dropped into the Slack channel.

Kira (Slack, 8:47 a.m.): "Hey, heads up. People are talking about Swaggernauts on Reddit now. There's a whole thread in r/Scrum. Might want to check it out."

Alex clicked the link. Five hundred comments.

"Has anyone used this 'Swaggernauts Guidebook' thing? Does it actually work?"

"Yeah, I tried it with my team. The WIP Limits are annoying at first, but it's wild how much cleaner the board gets."

"Is there a guide somewhere?"

Alex glanced at the screen, wide-eyed. "They're asking for guides now?"

Scaling the Legacy

One month later, Nathan pulled Alex into his office.

"It's time," Nathan said, folding his hands on the table. "The board wants to offer Swaggernauts' Guidebook as a public product."

Alex blinked. "What?"

"We're going to open-source it," Nathan said, nodding slowly. "We're going to publish it as a public guide."

Alex leaned back, stunned. "Why?"

Nathan tilted his head. "Because it's bigger than us now."

He tapped the desk. "People are talking about it. Companies are already copying it. If we release it as an official guidebook, we don't lose control—we become the source. The origin."

Alex leaned forward. "You're talking about legacy."

"Yes, I am," Nathan said, his eyes sharp. "Most people chase money or promotions. But systems? Systems live on. Systems outlast us."

Alex sat in silence for a moment, absorbing it all. Then she smiled. "Alright," Alex said. "Let's do it."

Open-Sourcing the Future

Tess, Ravi, and Alex sat in the team room, watching the recording of Nathan's announcement.

"Today, we're releasing the Swaggernauts Guidebook to the world. We're publishing the system that changed our company so it can change others, too."

Ravi leaned forward, eyes wide. "We're going open-source?"

Tess shifted her head. "Guess we really are the bar."

Alex sat quietly, eyes on the screen, watching the ripple they'd started grow into something far bigger than themselves.

They weren't just a team anymore.

They were the system.

Chapter 17 Summary

Chapter 17 showcases how Team Swaggernauts' journey evolves from a team transformation to a global influence, as their system garners widespread recognition and inspires Agile practitioners worldwide.

Key Developments

The Email That Starts It All

- Alex receives an invitation to discuss Team Swaggernauts' journey on *The Agile Mindset Podcast* after Nathan Cross's LinkedIn post positions the team as a standard of excellence.

The Podcast and Its Impact

- Alex's podcast appearance highlights the Swaggernauts' journey from dysfunction to creating a winning system, resonating with Agile professionals worldwide.
- The episode generates widespread interest, leading to requests from Scrum Masters, Agile Coaches, and executives eager to learn about the Swaggernauts Guidebook.

The World Takes Notice

- Online discussions, Reddit threads, and industry forums praise and debate the Swaggernauts' system, demonstrating its growing influence.
- Requests push the guidebook beyond internal use into a highly sought-after resource.

Scaling the System

- Nathan announces plans to open-source the Swaggernauts Guidebook, framing it as a contribution to the Agile and Scrum communities.
- Alex embraces the opportunity to shift from Scrum Master to global influence, recognizing the potential to inspire systemic change at scale.

Themes and Takeaways

The Power of Systems

- Sustainable systems, not individual efforts, drive long-term transformation by enabling scalability and resilience. Alex's shift from Scrum Master to influencing global practices demonstrates how effective systems can create far-reaching change.

Sharing Builds Influence

- Open-sourcing the Swaggernauts Guidebook ensures accessibility, enabling widespread adoption and empowering teams globally, reinforcing the influence of shared knowledge.

Conclusion

Chapter 17 solidifies Team Swaggernauts' legacy as a transformative force in Agile practices. By sharing their guidebook with the world, they extend their influence beyond their company, turning their journey into a global movement for teamwork and productivity.

Reflection Questions

- What behaviors do you consistently practice to maintain high performance in yourself and your team?
- How do you model balance and sustainability to ensure long-term success for your team?

Chapter 18

The Future:
From Team to Global Movement

One Year Later

It had been exactly one year since the Project UXcellence demo.

The team room looked the same but felt different. The desks, the chairs, and the whiteboard were still there. The hum of laptops, the quiet clicking of keyboards—all the same.

But something had shifted.

They weren't the same team anymore.

Tess sat at the front of the room, typing quietly. Her headphones were off, which was now usual. In the past, Tess wore her headphones like armor, blocking everything out. Now? She listened. She watched. She engaged.

"Ravi, you want eyes on this logic before I push it?" Tess asked, leaning her head back.

Ravi spun his chair around, grinning. "You're asking me to check your work?"

Tess shrugged, a small smile tugging at the corner of her lips. "Don't make me regret it, QA."

"Never," Ravi said, scooting over to her desk. "Run it one more time. Let's see if it holds up."

Visit from Nathan

At 10:15 a.m., Nathan walked in.

He wasn't wearing his usual button-down. He had on a simple black polo, with jeans. He walked like he didn't have a care in the world—but Alex knew better. Nathan never moved without purpose.

"Alright, team, listen up," Nathan said, clapping his hands together. Everyone stopped working.

"It's time," he said, glancing around the room. "Time to talk about the future. And I want Swaggernauts at the center of it."

Alex raised an eyebrow. "We're already at the center of it."

Nathan pointed at them. "Exactly. So, let's make it official."

He paced to the front of the room, tapping the whiteboard with a dry-erase marker. He wrote three big words: "Swaggernauts Institute."

The room went still.

Tess squinted. "What's that?"

Nathan turned, eyes sharp. "It's our next move."

Introducing the Swaggernauts Institute

"Here's the deal," Nathan began, tapping the words on the board. "The Swaggernauts Guidebook isn't just ours anymore. It's the industry's."

He stepped forward, hands in his pockets, his eyes scanning each of them in turn. "But people aren't just reading it. They want to learn from it. They want to connect with it. That's where the Swaggernauts Institute comes in."

Alex blinked slowly. "You're talking about more training and workshops, aren't you?"

"Exactly," Nathan replied, smiling. "Think public training sessions, but not for profit. We host open workshops, create free resources, and build a community around the system."

Ravi whirled his head. "Free?"

Nathan nodded. "Free. The goal isn't to monetize this. The Agile space doesn't need another certification. The goal is to make it even more accessible. This isn't about dollars; it's about impact."

Tess lifted her head back. "Oh no, this sounds like a lot of public-facing stuff. Please tell me I don't have to do speeches."

Nathan laughed. "No speeches, Tess. Just practical sessions—hands-on, interactive workshops where people can experience the system."

"Still sounds like speeches," Tess muttered.

The Reflection

That afternoon, the team stayed after hours. They didn't have to. They just did.

The whiteboard was full of notes about the Swaggernauts Institute. Roles, logistics, topics for workshops, and ideas for online resources. Everyone had added something to it.

At some point, Tess put the marker down, staring at the board.

"I still don't get it," she said, folding her arms. "We didn't do anything special."

Alex turned slowly. "What do you mean?"

"I mean…we didn't build anything. We didn't make an app. We didn't invent some tool. All we did was change how we work." Tess glanced at the board, shaking her head. "And now they want to give us a whole institute? For what?"

Alex walked up, uncapped the marker, and wrote two words at the top of the board: "The system."

"That's what we built, Tess," Alex said, turning toward her. "Not an app. Not a tool. An approach that transforms mindsets."

She underlined it twice. "You know what's more powerful than the latest new product? A mindset. Because a product lasts until someone builds something better. But a mindset? A mindset can last forever."

Tess tilted her head, thinking it over. "Alright," she muttered, nodding slowly. "I'll give you that."

How It All Changed

Later that evening, after the others had left, Alex stayed behind, sitting quietly at the table. Her laptop was open, but she wasn't typing.

She was thinking. Reflecting.

The whiteboard was still full of notes from the day's discussion. But one part stood out. It wasn't something she wrote. It was something Ravi wrote.

"Win together. Fail together."

Alex stared at it for a long time.

She remembered the first retro, when Tess finally admitted, "That's on me."

She remembered the first commitment, the first mob, the first win.

She remembered the first moment Tess called for help on her own.

This is what it means to win together, Alex thought.

She glanced at the empty seats where Tess, Ravi, and Kira usually sat. But they didn't feel empty anymore. They were full of something else.

Legacy.

The Interview

Two months later, Alex stood in front of a conference audience of four hundred Scrum Masters, Agile Coaches, and team leads.

Behind them, the big screen displayed a single image: The Swaggernauts Guidebook logo.

"Good morning, everyone," Alex began, stepping forward. "I'm here today to tell you a story. Not about a product. Not about a tool. But about a system. A system that didn't just change one team. It changed a company. And it's starting to change the industry."

She pointed at the screen behind them, where the four components were displayed:

Dynamic Fractals
WIP Limits
Teaming
Commitment Language

"This is the system," Alex said, pacing slowly. "But before I explain it, let me tell you about the first day it almost didn't work."

The crowd leaned in.

Legacy Secured

Eight months later, Nathan sent a message to the company Slack channel.

[8:15 a.m.] Nathan (CEO): "Big milestone today: We just hosted our Fiftieth Swaggernauts Guidebook workshop. Teams from thirty-five companies and eight countries participated. This isn't just ours anymore. It's the world's."

Where Are They Now?

- Tess became one of the lead trainers for the Swaggernauts Institute, hosting webinars on Swarming tactics. Her sessions were consistently rated five stars by attendees.
- Ravi shifted into a new role as a continuous improvement coach, helping other teams adopt Swarming, Pairing, and collective ownership.
- Kira became the director of product strategy for Agilion, pushing for more teams to adopt full WIP Limits for focus and Dynamic Fractals for shared responsibility.
- Alex became the executive director of the Swaggernauts Institute, leading public-facing efforts and guiding companies worldwide on how to transform their teams.

- Mateo joined the global community team for the Swaggernauts Institute, designing interactive case studies for workshops.
- Liam became an advocate for sustainable Agile practices, writing thought leadership articles and hosting panel discussions.
- Nia transitioned into a coaching role, focusing on creating psychological safety within teams to drive better collaboration.
- Ethan became a technical advisor for the Institute, designing frameworks for teams to measure the impact of their improvements.
- Harper took on a leadership role in the company's innovation lab, applying fractal principles to prototype and test new ideas.

The Final Marker

Back in the original team room, the whiteboard was blank, except for one phrase written in black marker.

"Win together. Fail together."

Alex stood quietly, hands in her pockets, gazing at it. Her reflection hovered in the glass window near it. She'd seen this room change. She'd seen the team change. But now, she realized it wasn't just the team. It was them. "Alright," Alex muttered, smiling to herself. "Let's raise the bar again."

Chapter 18 Summary

Chapter 18 delivers a powerful conclusion to Team Swaggernauts' journey, showing how their transformation has far-reaching effects on their company, the Agile community, and teams worldwide. A year after the pivotal Project UXcellence demo, their practices have evolved into a global movement, redefining what modern teamwork can achieve.

Key Developments

A Year of Transformation

- One year after the Project UXcellence demo, Team Swaggernauts has grown from a high-pressure team to leaders in fostering thriving teams across the organization and beyond.

The Swaggernauts Institute

- Nathan announces the creation of the Swaggernauts Institute, a nonprofit initiative designed to make the guidebook and its principles accessible worldwide through free workshops, online resources, and a collaborative community.

Scaling the Legacy

- The Swaggernauts Guidebook influences teams from thirty-five companies across eight countries in its first year of public availability.
- Alex and the team embrace new roles as educators and advocates, sharing their principles through events and workshops.

The Power of Mindset

- Tess reflects on their success, with Alex explaining that the guidebook's enduring impact lies in the mindset it fosters—collaboration, accountability, and adaptability.

Key Concepts

From Team to Institution

- The Swaggernauts Institute transforms their system into a global framework, institutionalizing principles that inspire systemic change across organizations.

Systems That Last

- Sustainable systems, rather than individual successes, become the defining feature of enduring impact.

Leadership Through Influence

- Alex evolves into a global advocate for collaboration, amplifying her leadership influence across industries and organizations.

Shared Accountability as a Movement

- "Win Together, Fail Together" transforms into a global movement, uniting teams under the shared power of collective accountability.

Themes and Takeaways

Sustainable Impact

- The Swaggernauts' system demonstrates adaptability, showing how robust principles drive lasting change across diverse contexts.

The Power of Collaboration

- Shared accountability and collective ownership with the F.I.T. Formula redefine global teamwork, setting a new standard for collaboration.

Impact Beyond Profit

- Through the nonprofit Swaggernauts Institute, the team prioritizes accessibility and transformation over profit, creating a model for mission-driven success.

From Local to Global

- The Swaggernauts Guidebook evolves into a global framework, shaping how organizations worldwide redefine collaboration and accountability.

Conclusion

Chapter 18 celebrates the culmination of Team Swaggernauts' journey, as their practices evolve into a global movement for transformation. Through the creation of the Swaggernauts Institute, their guidebook becomes a resource for teams worldwide, ensuring their principles endure. Their legacy lies not just in their accomplishments but in inspiring teams to adopt sustainable systems that prioritize shared success, proving that collaboration and accountability can transform the world of work.

Reflection Questions

- How do your current actions align with the legacy you want to leave within your organization or industry?
- What behaviors can you adopt today to inspire others to be their best?

Chapter 19

The F.I.T. Formula:
Why It Works

Expanding on the concepts behind the F.I.T. Formula, here's how the works of prominent scholars and authors directly support each component and the overall approach:

---

1. **Elinor Ostrom: Dynamic Fractals**

Elinor Ostrom's research on governing the commons (particularly in her book *Governing the Commons*) demonstrates how small, self-organizing groups can effectively manage shared resources. Her principles are directly relevant to Dynamic Fractals in the F.I.T. Formula:

1. **Clearly Defined Boundaries**: Dynamic Fractals create clear boundaries within a Scrum team by focusing on a single story or task. This clarity prevents overlapping responsibilities and fosters ownership.
2. **Collective Choice Arrangements**: By allowing teams to self-organize and decide how to structure their fractals, you empower members to take ownership of their workflow, increasing buy-in and engagement.
3. **Monitoring and Accountability**: Small groups naturally promote visibility and accountability. Ostrom found that peer monitoring in small communities reduces free riding, a concept akin to reducing social loafing in Scrum teams.

4. **Adaptive Structures**: Ostrom highlights how groups adapt their rules based on experience. Dynamic Fractals mirror this flexibility by reconfiguring themselves based on the evolving needs of the team and sprint goals.

How It Supports the F.I.T. Formula

Dynamic Fractals embody Ostrom's principles by leveraging small, accountable units that are empowered to govern themselves. This builds trust, encourages engagement, and mitigates challenges like social loafing.

---

2. Richard Hackman: Team Effectiveness and Conditions

Richard Hackman's research on team effectiveness, particularly in his book *Leading Teams: Setting the Stage for Great Performances*, identifies key conditions for team success that underpin the F.I.T. Formula.

1. **Enabling Structure:** Hackman emphasizes the role of structure in team effectiveness. Dynamic Fractals create a clear structure that fosters shared responsibility, while WIP Limits ensure the team maintains focus and avoids overcommitment.
2. **Compelling Direction:** Clear and achievable goals, such as those articulated through Commitment Language, align team efforts and provide a shared purpose, a core principle in Hackman's framework.
3. **Supportive Context:** Hackman highlights the importance of providing teams with the resources and environment needed to thrive. Teaming practices, such as Mobbing and Swarming, encourage collaboration and knowledge sharing, building a supportive team culture.
4. **Coaching for Growth:** Hackman identifies coaching as vital for continuous improvement. The iterative nature of the F.I.T. Formula, coupled with practices like retrospectives, creates a culture of learning and adaptation.

How It Supports the F.I.T. Formula

Hackman's insights validate the importance of creating structural, directional, and cultural conditions for team success. The F.I.T. Formula operationalizes these principles through its integrated system, fostering high performance and resilience.

---

3. Jeffrey Liker: WIP Limits of One Story at a Time

Jeffrey Liker's *The Toyota Way* emphasizes Lean principles, including limiting WIP to improve flow efficiency. WIP Limits ensure a clear focus, reduce waste, and enable teams to deliver faster and more predictably.

1. **Focus on Flow**: Lean systems, as described by Liker, prioritize the uninterrupted flow of work. Limiting WIP aligns with this principle, ensuring that Dynamic Fractals can focus on completing one story at a time without distractions.
2. **Reduce Multitasking**: Liker discusses the inefficiency caused by multitasking, a common issue in teams with excessive WIP. By limiting WIP, teams avoid task-switching and deliver higher-quality work.
3. **Visual Management**: Tools like Kanban boards, which Liker advocates, make WIP Limits visible. This transparency reinforces social accountability and helps teams stay aligned with their commitments.

How It Supports the F.I.T. Formula

WIP Limits, inspired by Lean principles, prevent overloading Dynamic Fractals and ensure that work progresses efficiently. This supports both individual focus and collective productivity.

---

4. Anita Woolley: Teaming

Anita Woolley's research on collective intelligence highlights how group performance depends on team dynamics rather than individual intelligence. Her findings reinforce the value of collaboration techniques like Pairing, Swarming, and Mobbing.

1. **Social Sensitivity**: Woolley's studies show that teams with high collective intelligence often exhibit strong social sensitivity—the ability to understand and adapt to others' perspectives. Techniques like Mobbing foster this sensitivity by requiring constant interaction and shared decision-making.

2. **Equal Participation**: High-performing teams balance contributions among members. Teaming techniques of Mobbing, Swarming, and Pairing ensure equal participation by design, as everyone is actively engaged in solving the same problem.

3. **Building Social Capital**: Frequent collaboration strengthens trust and relationships within the team, a critical component of social capital. Woolley's work emphasizes the importance of these factors in boosting team performance.

How It Supports the F.I.T. Formula

Collaboration techniques like Pairing and Mobbing build collective intelligence, which is essential for solving complex problems and fostering team cohesion.

---

5. Charles Duhigg and James Clear: Commitment Language and Micro-Habits

Both Charles Duhigg's *The Power of Habit* and James Clear's *Atomic Habits* delve into the science of habit formation, which underpins the concept of micro-commitments and Commitment Language.

1. **Cue-Routine-Reward Loop (Duhigg)**: Duhigg's habit loop explains how habits form through repeated cues, routines, and rewards. Using Commitment Language creates a cue (in the

Daily Scrum), a routine (making a public micro-commitment) and completing those commitments (reward) that reinforces accountability.

2. **The Power of Small Wins (Clear)**: Clear emphasizes the value of starting small. Micro-commitments—like promising to complete a single task or a part of a story—build momentum over time, leading to sustained progress.

3. **Identity-Based Habits (Clear)**: Clear argues that habits are more likely to stick when tied to identity. Using Commitment Language reinforces the team's identity as reliable, accountable, and high-performing.

How It Supports the F.I.T. Formula

Micro-commitments through Commitment Language leverage habit science to create a culture of accountability and continuous improvement, addressing challenges like low productivity and social loafing.

---

6. **Daniel Pink: Engagement and Autonomy**

   Daniel Pink's *Drive* identifies three key drivers of motivation:

   1. **Autonomy**: Dynamic Fractals and self-organization give team members the autonomy to decide how they work, which Pink identifies as critical for engagement.

   2. **Mastery**: Teaming techniques like Mobbing, Swarming, and Pairing offer opportunities for skill-building and cross-training, fostering a sense of mastery.

   3. **Purpose**: The formula aligns the team's efforts with clear goals, ensuring that their work feels purposeful and impactful.

How It Supports the F.I.T. Formula

Pink's framework ensures that the formula not only addresses productivity but also fosters intrinsic motivation, improving engagement and collaboration.

7. Robert Putnam: Social Capital and Collaboration

Robert Putnam's *Bowling Alone* explores the importance of social capital—trust, reciprocity, and shared norms—in building strong communities. This concept is vital for team collaboration.

1. **Trust and Reciprocity**: Dynamic Fractals and Teaming techniques build trust, which strengthens team cohesion.
2. **Shared Norms**: WIP Limits, Commitment Language, and micro-habits create shared norms that guide team behavior, enhancing accountability and collective ownership.

How It Supports the F.I.T. Formula

By fostering social capital, the formula improves collaboration and reduces issues like low interaction and poor engagement.

8. Peter Senge: Collective Ownership

Peter Senge's *The Fifth Discipline* emphasizes systems thinking and shared vision as keys to team success. Collective ownership is critical for aligning individual contributions with team goals.

1. **Shared Vision**: The formula's focus on Dynamic Fractals and WIP Limits ensures alignment with the sprint goal, creating a shared vision.
2. **Feedback Loops**: Retrospectives and Commitment Language create feedback loops that promote continuous learning and improvement.

How It Supports the F.I.T. Formula

Senge's insights ensure that the formula fosters a culture of shared responsibility and alignment.

9. Donella Meadows: Systems Thinking and Leverage

Donella Meadows' seminal work in systems thinking, particularly in her book *Thinking in Systems: A Primer*, highlights the interconnectedness of systems and the importance of identifying leverage points to create impactful change. Her insights resonate strongly with the F.I.T. Formula by emphasizing the necessity of systemic interventions rather than isolated fixes.

1. **Understanding Interconnections:** Meadows' systems thinking underscores how team dynamics are influenced by broader organizational structures. Dynamic Fractals and WIP Limits align with this by addressing interconnected issues of ownership and focus.

2. **Leverage Points:** Meadows highlights the importance of targeted interventions, such as WIP Limits and Commitment Language, which act as levers for systemic improvement. These levers not only address immediate team behaviors but also reshape underlying structures for sustainable change.

3. **Holistic Change:** Meadows' principles reinforce the F.I.T. Formula's emphasis on treating teams as systems where every component influences the whole. The formula integrates multiple levers—Dynamic Fractals for responsibility, Teaming for collaboration, WIP Limits for focus, and Commitment Language for accountability—to drive transformation.

How It Supports the F.I.T. Formula

Meadows' work inspires the systemic approach of the F.I.T. Formula, ensuring that each component addresses root causes and interacts synergistically to promote enduring team growth.

---

10. Patrick Lencioni: Five Dysfunctions of a Team Framework

The Five Dysfunctions of a Team framework by Patrick Lencioni provides another theoretical backbone that aligns well with the concepts and practices discussed in this book. Here's how each dysfunction connects to the formula:

1. **Absence of Trust**

   Related Concepts: Dynamic Fractals and Teaming

   - **Dysfunction Insight**: Teams that lack trust avoid vulnerability, which hinders their ability to admit mistakes or ask for help.
   - **How the F.I.T. Formula Solves It**
     - Dynamic Fractals, combined with practices like Mobbing and Swarming, create a safe environment where vulnerability is normalized.
     - Small teams inherently foster higher trust due to their intimate structure.
     - Teaming techniques strengthen interpersonal bonds, making it easier for team members to rely on and trust one another.

2. **Fear of Conflict**

   Related Concepts: Dynamic Fractals, Teaming, and Commitment Language

   - **Dysfunction Insight**: Teams avoid constructive debates, resulting in surface-level agreements without real resolution. This often stems from a lack of trust, discomfort with vulnerability, and a fear of damaging relationships. Avoiding conflict may feel easier in the short term, but it leads to poor decisions, unresolved tensions, and a lack of genuine collaboration.
   - **How the F.I.T. Formula Solves It**
     - By working in small, Dynamic Fractals, team members interact closely and frequently. These intimate settings create a space where people feel safer to express concerns, challenge ideas, or admit when something doesn't make sense.
     - Teaming creates real-time collaboration where people work together. The constant interaction

fosters a culture where disagreements are seen as problem-solving opportunities rather than personal attacks. Teaming ensures that different perspectives are aired immediately, reducing the buildup of unresolved conflict.

- Commitment Language requires explicit, measurable commitments during Daily Scrums, ensuring disagreements surface early when discussing achievable goals. These structured conversations encourage constructive dialogue and prevent underlying tensions from festering.

3. **Lack of Commitment**

Related Concepts: WIP Limits, Commitment Language, and micro-habits

- **Dysfunction Insight**: Without clarity and buy-in, team members are noncommittal, leading to ambiguity about priorities and responsibilities.
- **How the F.I.T. Formula Solves It**
  - WIP Limits ensure that the team focuses on completing one story at a time, eliminating overcommitment and fostering clarity.
  - By articulating clear, measurable commitments during Daily Scrums, team members shift from passive "I'll try" statements to proactive "We will" declarations. This reinforces ownership of goals and ensures team alignment toward achieving objectives.
  - Micro-habits, like small, daily wins, build momentum and reinforce a culture of following through on commitments.

4. **Avoidance of Accountability**

Related Concepts: Peer Accountability in Dynamic Fractals and Commitment Language

- **Dysfunction Insight**: Teams hesitate to hold each other accountable, leading to declining performance.

- **How the F.I.T. Formula Solves It**
  - Dynamic Fractals create clear boundaries of ownership within teams. Peer monitoring within these small, Dynamic Fractals ensures that accountability happens naturally, without the need for external intervention. The fractal collectively owns the work, reducing social loafing and encouraging mutual responsibility.
  - The act of publicly stating commitments during Daily Scrums fosters peer accountability. When commitments are made visible, team members feel a stronger obligation to deliver, knowing their peers depend on their contributions.

5. **Inattention to Results**

   Related Concepts: Shared vision, feedback loops, and Commitment Language

   - **Dysfunction Insight**: Teams prioritize personal success or departmental wins over collective outcomes.
   - **How the F.I.T. Formula Solves It**
     - Shared sprint goals, facilitated by Dynamic Fractals and WIP Limits, align individual efforts with the team's objectives.
     - Regular retrospectives and real-time feedback loops (e.g., during Mobbing or Swarming) create opportunities for the team to reflect on what's working and what isn't. By focusing on the work rather than the individual, these discussions encourage open feedback without fear of personal judgment.
     - Clear, daily commitments tie individual actions to collective outcomes, ensuring the team stays focused on achieving measurable, shared goals. The process of articulating commitments makes results tangible, fostering a shared sense of purpose.

The Five Dysfunctions framework provides a lens to understand the cultural and psychological challenges addressed by the F.I.T. formula. By embedding practices that counteract these dysfunctions, your approach ensures teams not only operate efficiently but also thrive in terms of trust, engagement, and alignment.

Each section of the formula is strongly supported by these foundational works, weaving together concepts from social science, Lean principles, behavioral psychology, and Agile frameworks.

Recap

How the Formula Transformed Team Swaggernauts for Lasting Success

Starting Stuck

At the beginning of the journey, Team Swaggernauts was like many Scrum teams—stuck. Their workflow board was a mess of half-finished stories. Stories lingered in the "In Progress" column for days, sometimes weeks. Team members worked in isolation, operating like individual contributors rather than a unified team. Social loafing was rampant, and everyone was "waiting on someone else" to finish their part.

This wasn't because they were lazy. It wasn't because they lacked talent. It was because the system they were working in was broken.

Scrum theory suggests that teams should be self-organizing, collaborative, and focused on delivering a "Done" increment each sprint. But the reality for Team Swaggernauts was far from that ideal. Their structure encouraged multitasking, isolated work, and shallow accountability.

The system needed to change. And that change required more than tools, templates, or rules. It required a complete transformation of how the team worked together.

How the F.I.T. Formula Transformed Team Swaggernauts

When the team adopted the F.I.T. Formula, they experienced a shift that wasn't just procedural—it was transformational. This shift wasn't just about checking off new tasks or following a new set of rules. It was about changing how they approached teamwork, ownership, and accountability.

The formula has four key components, and each one contributed to their success in a unique way:

---

1. **Dynamic Fractals (Breaking Down Silos, Building Ownership)**

Problem Before the Formula

The team worked as a large, loose group. Each member had their own "personal workload," and when things got stuck, everyone waited for someone else to act. Ownership was fragmented, and tasks got lost in handoffs.

The Shift

With Dynamic Fractals, the large team of nine engineers was broken into three fractals of three people each. These three-person fractals worked on only one story at a time. Each Dynamic Fractal had complete ownership over their story.

The Impact

This simple change did two powerful things:
- It eliminated handoffs. The people who started a story were the same people who finished it.
- It built shared ownership. Since the fractal succeeded or failed together, they stopped thinking in terms of "my part" and started thinking in terms of "our story."

Supporting Theory

This approach is rooted in the work of Elinor Ostrom and her principles of collective ownership and self-governance. By giving small, Dynamic Fractals control over a complete story, the team applied one of Ostrom's key principles: "Those who are affected by rules should be part of making the rules." This created a sense of ownership and commitment. It also drew on the concept of "social capital," as highlighted by Robert Putnam in *Bowling Alone*, which underscores the importance of trust, norms, and networks in fostering collaboration. Since team members had to work closely within their fractal, they began building trust and accountability with each other. Additionally, Donella Meadows' systems thinking underscores the importance of structure as a leverage point for behavioral change. Finally, Richard Hackman's research on team effectiveness emphasizes the value of clear structures in enabling teams to align their efforts and build cohesion, which is precisely what fractals achieve.

---

2. WIP Limits (Focus, Flow, and Faster Delivery)

Problem Before the Formula

At any given moment, Team Swaggernauts had nine or more stories in progress. Everyone was juggling multiple tasks, constantly switching contexts. This caused delays, confusion, and cognitive overload. People "looked busy," but nothing was getting done.

The Shift

The team implemented a WIP Limit of one story per Dynamic Fractal. Instead of every person working on "their own task," Dynamic Fractals collectively worked on just one story at a time. The goal was simple: finish what you start.

The Impact

This change led to a major shift in velocity and focus. Stories didn't linger for weeks. Stories moved from "In Progress" to "Done" quickly. People didn't feel overwhelmed, and progress became visible and tangible.

Supporting Theory

This shift is grounded in Lean and Flow Theory, as popularized by thinkers like Don Reinertsen and David Anderson (creator of the Kanban method). The concept of limiting WIP reduces cognitive load (as defined by John Sweller's theory of cognitive load) and ensures that attention is focused on fewer tasks at once. This prevents multitasking, which research has shown to reduce productivity. Donella Meadows' leverage points remind us that constraints, such as WIP Limits, can change how the work moves through a system, creating focus and reducing waste. By limiting WIP, Team Swaggernauts created an environment where flow was more important than activity.

---

3. **Teaming (Mobbing, Swarming, Pairing)**

Problem Before the Formula

When team members got "stuck," they stayed stuck. They didn't ask for help because it was seen as a sign of weakness or as "bothering other people." Tasks would sit idle for days while people worked on other "easier" stories.

The Shift

The team adopted collaboration techniques like Swarming, Pairing, and Mobbing. The idea was simple: when someone is stuck, everyone swarms the problem. Dynamic Fractals didn't wait for formal Daily Scrums to ask for help. They called for help immediately within their fractal and if necessary, the whole team with fractal-to-fractal Teaming. Thus, the fractal and the whole team worked as a unit to resolve issues in real-time.

The Impact

Blockers didn't last for days anymore. Issues were resolved within hours. The team's sense of urgency increased, and team members began to rely on one another more deeply. Swarming wasn't just a productivity tool—it became part of the team's social norm.

Supporting Theory

This concept is supported by Amy Edmondson's work on *Teaming*. Edmondson's research on psychological safety shows that teams are more effective when people feel safe to ask for help. Swarming reinforces this principle because it encourages people to say, "I'm stuck" and then get immediate help. Richard Hackman's findings highlight the importance of interdependence in team success; Swarming amplifies this by making collaboration the default behavior. Anita Woolley's research on collective intelligence further emphasizes how effective teamwork arises from the ability of groups to leverage diverse perspectives and skills, which is precisely what Swarming achieves. By fostering real-time collaboration, Swarming enables teams to solve problems faster and more effectively than individuals working in isolation.

---

4. **Commitment Language (Accountability, Micro-Habits, and Social Contracts)**

Problem Before the Formula

Sprint commitments were vague. Team members said things like, "I'll try to get that done," or "I'll see what I can do." There was no firm accountability, and it was unclear if anyone truly owned a task.

The Shift

With the new system, team members stopped saying "I'll try" and started saying "We will." Fractals made micro-commitments daily. Instead of setting broad sprint goals, they made small, daily commitments, like "We will finish story #14 by noon today." This shift created accountability and urgency.

The Impact

Micro-commitments turned abstract "intentions" into concrete actions. When people knew they had made a commitment to their peers, they followed through. It created a social contract. Instead of "trying to get things done," they did them.

Supporting Theory

This approach draws on principles from David Marquet's work in *Turn the Ship Around.* Marquet's system of using "intent-based leadership" encouraged people to shift from passive followers to active leaders. By making daily commitments, team members took ownership of outcomes, not just tasks. Donella Meadows' insight into reinforcing feedback loops also aligns with the concept of Commitment Language—small, consistent commitments create a positive feedback loop that builds trust and momentum. Additionally, the work of Charles Duhigg in *The Power of Habit* and James Clear in *Atomic Habits* highlights how micro-habits and incremental changes can lead to profound, long-term transformation. This approach further taps into behavioral science concepts like commitment devices, which are shown to increase follow-through and create lasting change. Commitment devices are tools, strategies, or structures that help individuals follow through on their intentions by increasing the cost of failure or making success more likely.

The Results

Before the Formula:

- Stories lingered for weeks.
- Blockers lasted for days.
- People worked on isolated tasks instead of collaborating.
- Accountability was low and progress was slow.

After the Formula:

- Stories were completed daily, not weekly.
- Blockers were resolved in hours, not days.
- Dynamic Fractals co-owned every story, building shared responsibility.
- Team members made concrete daily commitments to each other and social accountability replaced social loafing.

How the Formula Achieved True Transformational Change

Many teams chase transactional change—small, surface-level adjustments like switching tools or updating processes. But Team Swaggernauts achieved transformational change.

Here's how the Formula achieved it:

- It didn't just adjust team behavior. It changed team beliefs.
- It didn't create new superficial rules. It created new social norms.
- It didn't treat visible symptoms like "blockers" or "velocity." It treated root causes like accountability, collaboration, and ownership.

By the end of the journey, Team Swaggernauts wasn't just delivering faster—they had become a different kind of team, one with clarity, urgency, and unity.

This is the power of the F.I.T. Formula. It's not about process tweaks. It's about redesigning the system. It's about creating teams that don't plateau.

If you want to experience this transformation for your own team, the path is clear. Apply the F.I.T. Formula. Let Dynamic Fractals, WIP Limits, Teaming, and Commitment Language transform your team from "good" to great.

Conclusion

As you close this book, my hope is that you feel empowered to transform the way your teams operate, lead, and succeed. Whether you're a Scrum Master striving for better sprint outcomes, an Agile Coach supporting team-wide adoption, or a Product Owner aligning priorities to business goals, the F.I.T. Formula provides the framework to move from reactive problem-solving to proactive excellence.

This book is for those who see the potential in their teams and are ready to take the next step. It's a call to action for anyone who believes that accountability, collaboration, focus, and ownership aren't just ideals but attainable realities. The journey of the Swaggernauts illustrates that change isn't easy, but it's always worth it.

By integrating Dynamic Fractals for ownership, WIP Limits for focus, Teaming for collaboration, and Commitment Language for accountability, you now have a roadmap to guide your teams toward meaningful and lasting improvement. Remember, excellence isn't a destination—it's a system. And when that system works, it creates ripple effects that extend far beyond the team.

Thank you for joining this journey. Now, take these tools, adapt them to your context, and lead the change you want to see. Together, we can keep raising the bar.

References

1. Anderson, David J.
   Kanban: Successful Evolutionary Change for Your Technology Business. Blue Hole Press, 2010.
   (Referenced for Kanban Boards, WIP Limits, and visual management tools.)
2. Beck, Kent, et al.
   Manifesto for Agile Software Development. Agile Alliance, 2001.
   (Cited for definitions of Agile and Scrum.)
3. Clear, James.
   Atomic Habits: An Easy & Proven Way to Build Good Habits & Break Bad Ones. Avery, 2018.
   (Cited for Micro-Habits and building momentum through small wins.)
4. Duhigg, Charles.
   The Power of Habit: Why We Do What We Do in Life and Business. Random House Trade Paperbacks, 2014.
   (Referenced for Micro-Commitments and habit formation.)
5. Edmondson, Amy C.
   Teaming: How Organizations Learn, Innovate, and Compete in the Knowledge Economy. Jossey-Bass, 2012.
   (Referenced for Psychological Safety, Teaming, and Swarming.)
6. Hackman, J. Richard.
   Leading Teams: Setting the Stage for Great Performances. Harvard Business Review Press, 2002.
   (Cited for his framework on team effectiveness, including enabling structure, compelling direction, and supportive context.)

7. Larman, Craig, and Bas Vodde.
    Scaling Lean & Agile Development: Thinking and Organizational Tools for Large-Scale Scrum. Addison-Wesley, 2008.
    (Referenced for scaling Agile practices and team collaboration.)

8. Lencioni, Patrick.
    The Five Dysfunctions of a Team: A Leadership Fable. Jossey-Bass, 2002.
    (Cited for understanding barriers like Absence of Trust and Fear of Conflict.)

9. Liker, Jeffrey K.
    The Toyota Way: 14 Management Principles from the World's Greatest Manufacturer. McGraw-Hill Education, 2004.
    (Referenced for WIP Limits, Flow, and Lean principles.)

10. Marquet, L. David.
    Turn the Ship Around!: A True Story of Turning Followers Into Leaders. Portfolio, 2013.
    (Cited for Commitment Language and intent-based leadership.)

11. Meadows, Donella H.
    Thinking in Systems: A Primer. Chelsea Green Publishing, 2008.
    (Referenced for Systems Thinking and identifying leverage points to drive systemic change.)

12. Ostrom, Elinor.
    Governing the Commons: The Evolution of Institutions for Collective Action. Cambridge University Press, 1990.
    (Cited for Dynamic Fractals, collective governance, and accountability.)

13. Pink, Daniel H.
    Drive: The Surprising Truth About What Motivates Us. Riverhead Books, 2009.
    (Referenced for Autonomy, Mastery, and Purpose in fostering engagement and intrinsic motivation.)

14. Putnam, Robert D.
    Bowling Alone: The Collapse and Revival of American Community.

Simon & Schuster, 2000.

(Referenced for Social Capital and its impact on collaboration.)

15. Reinertsen, Donald G.

    The Principles of Product Development Flow: Second Generation Lean Product Development. Celeritas Publishing, 2009.

    (Cited for Lean principles and WIP management.)

16. Senge, Peter M.

    The Fifth Discipline: The Art and Practice of the Learning Organization. Currency Doubleday, 1990.

    (Referenced for Systems Thinking and Shared Vision.)

17. Sweller, John.

    Cognitive Load Theory. Psychology Press, 2011.

    (Cited for reducing cognitive overload through focused work and WIP Limits.)

18. Woolley, Anita W., et al.

    "Evidence for a Collective Intelligence Factor in the Performance of Human Groups." *Science,* vol. 330, no. 6004, 2010, pp. 686–688.

    (Referenced for Collective Intelligence, Social Sensitivity, and Collaboration Techniques.)

Appendices

Dynamic Fractals: What They Do

- **What Dynamic Fractals Provide**: They create structure by breaking a team into smaller, cross-functional sub-teams focused on a single story at a time. This structural framework is what enables fractals to work together and own outcomes.
- What Dynamic Fractals Enable
  1. **Shared Responsibility**: The fractal takes responsibility for completing the story together, reducing silos and finger-pointing.
  2. **Collective Ownership**: The outcome of shared responsibility is that the fractal feels collective ownership of the story or outcome.

The Lever: Structure

Structure is the enabling mechanism that facilitates shared responsibility and leads to collective ownership. Without the structural organization of fractals, the shared responsibility and ownership wouldn't materialize.

Leverage Outcomes

- **Structure**: The structural framework provided by Dynamic Fractals sets the stage for everything that follows. It organizes how work is divided and facilitates collaboration.

- **Responsibility**: Shared responsibility is the immediate effect of working within the fractal structure. It's the "muscle" teams exercise to move toward ownership.
- **Ownership**: Ownership is the ultimate outcome—a team takes full accountability for their success or failure as fractals.

Appendix II:
WIP Limits Summary Sheet

WIP Limits: What They Do

- **What WIP Limits Provide**: WIP Limits constrain the number of stories a fractal and team can work on simultaneously. This ensures work is finished before new stories are started. WIP Limits eliminate distractions and encourage deep work, which is central to achieving focus.
- **What WIP Limits Enable**
    1. **Focus**: By limiting work in progress, teams prioritize finishing over starting, avoiding distractions and context-switching.
    2. **Flow**: Constraining work in progress enables a steady and predictable flow of work.
    3. **Quality**: Teams dedicate their energy to completing fewer tasks at a higher standard.
- Without focus, flow would be unpredictable, and quality would suffer. Flow and quality are natural consequences of focus.

The Lever: Focus

Focus is the direct result of limiting work in progress. WIP Limits force the team to prioritize and concentrate on completing tasks rather than juggling too many at once.

Leverage Outcomes

- **Focus**: WIP Limits encourage focus by narrowing the team's attention to the most important tasks. This prevents overwhelm and scattered efforts.
- **Flow**: The practical outcome of focus is smoother, more predictable workflow and faster task completion.
- **Quality**: The improved focus and flow translate into higher-quality deliverables.

Appendix III:
Teaming Summary Sheet

Teaming: What They Do

- **What Teaming Provides**: Teaming introduces collaborative practices like Mobbing, Swarming, and Pairing, where members work together in real-time to solve problems, complete stories, or remove blockers.
- **What Teaming Enables**
    1. **Cohesion**: Teaming strengthens interpersonal relationships, fostering trust, mutual reliance, and psychological safety.
    2. **Collaboration**: It enhances the team's ability to work together effectively by aligning efforts and sharing expertise.
    3. **Speed and Problem-Solving**: Real-time collaboration accelerates progress, removes blockers faster, and improves decision-making.
- Without collaboration, teams would struggle to achieve the same level of efficiency and alignment.

The Lever: Collaboration

Collaboration drives the process of real-time problem-solving and alignment. Collaboration is the means through which teams achieve cohesion, speed, and shared ownership.

Leverage Outcomes

- **Cohesion**: Teaming creates tight bonds among team members, improving trust and their ability to work seamlessly together.
- **Collaboration**: Collaboration is both an outcome and a process fostered by the mechanics of Mobbing, Swarming, and Pairing.
- **Shared Ownership**: By working together closely, teams take collective responsibility for stories and outcomes, improving accountability and alignment.

Appendix IV:
Commitment Language Summary Sheet

Commitment Language: What They Do

- **What Commitment Language Provides**: Commitment Language is designed to shift behavior from vague communication and task management (e.g., "I'm working on it") to specific, measurable, and actionable daily commitments made public during standups.
- **What Commitment Language Enables**
    1. **Accountability**: Team members publicly commit to what they will accomplish, creating a sense of personal ownership over outcomes.

2. **Alignment**: Ensures everyone understands individual contributions to the team's goals, reducing ambiguity and miscommunication.
3. **Transparency**: Creates visibility into what each team member is working on and allows the team to address blockers proactively.
4. **Momentum**: Builds a sense of progress as commitments are reviewed and achieved daily, driving the team forward.

Without accountability, these outcomes would be inconsistent or unattainable.

The Lever: Accountability

Accountability helps people take ownership of their commitments and follow through. Accountability is what ensures progress and alignment within the team.

Leverage Outcomes

- **Accountability**: Commitment Language directly reinforces personal and team accountability by tying specific actions to measurable results.
- **Clarity**: Clear and actionable commitments ensure that everyone understands expectations, reducing miscommunication and ambiguity.
- **Transparency**: The public nature of commitments fosters trust and collaboration, as everyone's work becomes visible.

Appendix V:
Sprint Planning Template

Purpose: Ensure alignment and clarity during sprint planning sessions.

Item	Detail		
Sprint Goal	Improve subscription management UX		
Committed Stories for Sprint	#15, #16, #17, #18, #19, #20, #21, #22, #23, #24		
Fractal A Assignment, Commitments, & Story Points	Tess, Ravi, Amina	#16, #18, #19	9
Fractal B Assignment, Commitments, & Story Points	Liam, Sofia, Mateo	#15, #21, #20, #24	10
Fractal C Assignment, Commitments, & Story Points	Nia, Ethan, Harper	#17, #23, #22	8

Appendix VI:
Commitment Language Example Template
for Daily Scrum

Purpose: Provide example language for use in a Daily Scrum. See center column.

Category	Example Language	Purpose
Individual Commitment (Reviewing Previous Commitment)	"Yesterday, I committed to completing the front-end logic for the subscription form and I finished it."	Ensures accountability by reviewing progress on past commitments and setting clear next steps.
Individual Commitment (New Commitment)	"Today, I commit to writing and unit testing the validation logic for the checkout process by the end of the day."	Provides clarity on specific, achievable goals for the day.
Fractal Commitment (Reviewing Previous Commitment)	"Our fractal committed to finalizing story #14 yesterday. We encountered a blocker but mobbed it and completed the task this morning."	Demonstrates shared accountability and progress review as a team.
Fractal Commitment (New Commitment)	"Today, our fractal commits to completing regression tests for story #15 and preparing it for review by the end of the day."	Aligns the fractal on a clear, shared goal, fostering collaboration and focus.

Best Practices for Daily Scrum Commitment Language

1. **Always Review Yesterday's Commitments**
   - Acknowledge what was completed, what remains, and any blockers encountered.
2. **Be Clear and Measurable**
   - Use specific language to define what success looks like for the day.
3. **Emphasize Ownership**
   - Use "I commit" for individual tasks and "We commit" for fractal tasks to highlight personal and collective accountability.
4. **Keep It Actionable**
   - Focus on tasks that can realistically be completed within the day's work timeframe.
5. **Keep It Positive and Safe**
   - Celebrate the completion of commitments.
   - Unmet commitments are an opportunity for transparency, vulnerability, and learning. Do admonish missed commitments.

Appendix VII:
Daily Scrum Commitment Tracker Template

Purpose: Record commitments, blockers, and progress over time for reference.

Team Member	Yesterday's Commitment	Yesterday's Results	Today's Commitment	Blockers
Tess	"Finalize API request logic"	Met *Celebrate*	"Deploy API changes to staging"	"Infrastructure team making updates to staging environment"
Ravi	"Run regression tests on story #12"	Met *Celebrate*	"Complete story #15 regression tests"	"Dependency on backend fix"
Scrum Master	"Connect with Scrum Master from Team Orion to align on dependency for the API integration."	Met *Celebrate*	"Escalate API access issue to infrastructure team lead and schedule resolution meeting before 11 a.m."	"SM from Team Orion previously on PTO"
Product Owner	"Get two stories ready for the team backlog refinement by 3 p.m."	Unmet *Discuss*	"Resolve outstanding compliance requirements question for new subscription flow."	"Waiting on Marketing and Legal to review new subscription flow"

The Scrum Master commitment highlights the typical responsibility in addressing external dependencies that might impede the team's progress, ensuring that blockers outside the team's control are managed effectively.

The Product Owner commitments reflect the typical focus on maintaining clarity, alignment, and prioritization for the team while actively working to remove uncertainties.

Avoid these weak/vague words and phrases:

"I worked on story X."	"I'll work on story X."	"I'll continue to work on…"
"I did work on story X."	"I'm going to do work on…"	"I'm going to do story X."
"I wrote code for story X."	"I started coding."	"I'll continue coding story X."
"I tested story X."	"I started testing."	"I'll continue testing story X."
"I hope to…"	"I should…"	"I might…"
"I'll try…"	"I'll likely…"	"I could…"
"I guess…"	"I suppose…"	"I'm not sure…"
"Potentially"	"Probably"	"Possibly"
"Perhaps"	"Hopefully"	"Maybe"
"If nothing happens…"	"If everything goes right…"	"I'll get X% done."

Example Language Script

1. "[I/We] [did/did not] meet [my/our] prior commitment. [I/We] accomplished _____ or [I/We] did not accomplish _____ because…"

2. "Today, [I/We] will accomplish _____ for the team." Or "To-day, [I/We] commit to…"

3. "[I/We] do not have any roadblocks" or "_____ is preventing [me/us] from accomplishing _____ for the team."
4. (Optional) After everyone has made their commitments, quick brief-backs can be utilized: "Today, [I/We] commit to _____."

Note: The optional brief-back is simply a restatement and is used at the end of the Daily Scrum. It provides the following benefits:

- Serves as a final opportunity to inspect and adapt a commitment, especially to support another team member or fractal after the original commitment was given.
- Reinforces verbally what was previously committed, minimizing forgetfulness.
- If the commitment is fractal-based, it gives another fractal member an opportunity to restate, which ensures alignment within the fractal. Tess states; Ravi briefs back.

Appendix VIII:
Teaming Technique Table

Aspect	Mobbing	Swarming	Pairing
Definition	The entire fractal or team working together on one task at the same time, sharing one keyboard and screen.	The entire fractal works on different tasks for the same story simultaneously to accelerate progress.	Two team members work together on a single task, alternating between driving and navigating.
Tasks	Focuses on one task at a time.	Divides multiple tasks related to one story or goal.	Focuses on one task at a time.
Keyboards	One keyboard shared among the group.	Multiple keyboards, one per person or task.	One keyboard shared between the pair.
Screens	One shared screen (physically or virtually).	Multiple screens, one per individual.	One shared screen (physically or virtually).
Roles	Rotating roles (e.g., driver, navigator, observers).	Roles are task-specific, with individuals taking ownership of subtasks.	Alternating roles: driver (types) and navigator (guides).
Collaboration Level	Very High: Entire fractal or team collaborates on the same task.	High: Collaboration occurs through coordination of related tasks.	Very High: Close, continuous collaboration between the pair.

Best For	Complex, critical tasks requiring diverse perspectives or brainstorming.	Stories with multiple independent subtasks that can be worked on in parallel.	Tasks requiring detailed attention or mentoring (e.g., code reviews, debugging).
Knowledge Sharing	Maximizes knowledge sharing across the team.	Moderate knowledge sharing within the team.	Excellent for deep knowledge sharing between two people.
Efficiency	Can be slower for simple tasks but ensures high quality and shared understanding.	Fast progress on stories with multiple subtasks but requires effective coordination.	Efficient for focused, detail-oriented tasks or skill transfer.
Examples	Debugging a critical bug, designing a complex feature, or brainstorming.	Working on multiple tasks within a single story, such as coding, testing, and documentation simultaneously.	Refactoring code, solving a tough bug, or mentoring a junior developer.

- **Mobbing** is ideal for highly collaborative tasks where the entire fractal's input is valuable.
- **Swarming** is best for accelerating progress on complex stories with many parts.
- **Pairing** focuses on deeper collaboration between two members for skill transfer or high-attention tasks.

Glossary of Terms

Agile: Mindset and methodology emphasizing iterative development, collaboration, and responsiveness to change, particularly through frameworks like Scrum.

Agile Coach: Coach, facilitator, and mentor who supports teams, leaders, and organizations in adopting Agile practices, fostering collaboration, continuous improvement, and alignment with Agile principles.

Backlog: Prioritized list of work items that the team needs to complete. Includes features, bugs, and technical work. Typically divided into a product backlog (long-term items) and a sprint backlog (items for the current sprint).

Blocker: Problem or issue that prevents a team or individual from making progress on a task. Blockers are addressed during Swarming sessions or Daily Scrum.

Cognitive Load: Mental effort required to process information and complete tasks. High cognitive load can reduce focus and decision-making capacity.

Commitment Language: Practice where team members make explicit, measurable commitments to their peers during Daily Scrum, fostering accountability.

Daily Scrum: Short, time-boxed meeting where team members share progress, blockers, and next steps. Also called a daily stand-up or stand-up.

Dynamic Fractals: Small, self-organizing sub-teams within a Scrum team, consisting of three to four members. Each fractal focuses on a single story or task, ensuring clear ownership and eliminating hand-offs. Fractals may dynamically adjust their member composition each sprint based upon sprint goals, technical interests, cross-training needs, desires to work with others, and work demands. In Agile, fractals are typically associated with scaling patterns outward from the team. In the context of the F.I.T. Formula, Dynamic Fractals represent 'inward scaling'—focusing on structuring for accountability, collaboration, focus, and ownership within the team itself.

Feedback Loops: Mechanisms to provide regular input and adapt processes, ensuring continuous improvement and alignment with goals. Examples include retrospectives and Swarming sessions.

Fractals: See Dynamic Fractals.

Fractals in Nature: Fractals in nature are self-similar recursive patterns, like tree branches, river networks, and snowflakes, that repeat at different scales, reflecting the underlying efficiency and order of natural processes.

Intrinsic Motivation: Motivation driven by internal factors such as personal satisfaction, mastery, and purpose, rather than external rewards or punishment.

Kanban Board: Visual tool used to track work items through various stages, such as "To Do," "In Progress," and "Done." Commonly used to implement WIP Limits. Sometimes referred to as a Scrum Board.

Lean Principles: Philosophy originating from Toyota's manufacturing system, emphasizing waste reduction, continuous improvement, and optimizing flow.

Micro-Commitments: Small, actionable promises made by team members to complete a task or deliverable within a short time frame. Expressed in the form of Commitment Language. Micro-commitments build momentum and trust within the team.

Mobbing: Teaming technique where the entire team focuses on solving a single problem or completing one task together, leveraging collective intelligence.

Multitasking: Practice of working on multiple tasks simultaneously, often leading to reduced focus and productivity. The F.I.T. Formula discourages multitasking by implementing WIP Limits.

Pairing: Teaming technique where two team members work together in real-time on the same task, ensuring shared knowledge and mutual accountability.

Parkinson's Law: The principle that work expands to fill the time available for its completion, highlighting the importance of clear deadlines and efficient planning.

Product Owner (PO): A key Scrum role responsible for maximizing the value of the product by managing the product backlog and ensuring clear communication of priorities to the team.

Psychological Safety: A team environment where members feel safe to take risks, voice ideas, and admit mistakes without fear of judgment.

Retrospective: Structured meeting held at the end of each sprint to reflect on what went well, what didn't, and how the team can improve.

Scrum: Agile framework for managing complex projects. It divides work into time-boxed iterations called sprints, emphasizing collaboration, flexibility, and delivery of value.

Scrum Master (SM): Facilitator and coach for the Scrum team, responsible for ensuring the team adheres to Scrum principles and practices.

Self-Organizing Teams: Teams that decide internally how to accomplish their work, leveraging their collective skills and expertise without micromanagement.

Shared Vision: Collective understanding and alignment among team members about the goals and purpose of their work.

Shu, Ha, Ri: Japanese concept describing stages of learning:

- **Shu (Follow):** Strictly follow foundational rules to build a strong base.

- **Ha (Break):** Adapt and innovate based on experience and understanding.

- **Ri (Master):** Operate with mastery, creativity, and independence, transcending the original framework.

Shu, Ha, Ri in Agile: A Japanese concept describing stages of learning: Shu (following rules), Ha (breaking and adapting rules), and Ri (creating new approaches). Teams may adopt a Shu stance during initial implementation of new practices for consistency.

Social Accountability: The sense of responsibility team members feel toward each other when commitments are made publicly, enhancing follow-through and collaboration.

Social Capital: The trust, mutual understanding, and shared values that enable effective collaboration within a team. Created through sharing information, generating collective output greater than the sum of the individual parts, offering mutual aid to one another, and turning an "I" mentality into a "we" mentality.

Social Loafing: Phenomenon where individuals put in less effort when working in a group, assuming others will pick up the slack. Addressed through Dynamic Fractals and Commitment Language in the F.I.T. Formula.

Social Norms: Shared expectations within a team regarding acceptable behaviors and practices that promote accountability and cohesion.

Sprint: Time-boxed period, typically one to four weeks, during which a Scrum team completes a set of work items.

Story: Small, user-focused work item that represents a piece of functionality or value to be delivered by the team.

Swarming: Teaming technique where multiple team members focus on resolving a single problem, like a story, by tackling multiple tasks in parallel in real-time.

System Thinking: Holistic approach to understanding how different components of a team or organization interact and influence each other.

Teaming: Collaboration techniques such as Mobbing, Swarming, and Pairing, where team members work together on a task in real-time to deliver efficiently or resolve blockers.

Transactional Change: Incremental adjustments to tools, processes, or workflows without addressing deeper systemic issues or team culture.

Transformational Change: Comprehensive changes that redefine a team's culture, collaboration, and approach to work, leading to lasting improvement.

Velocity: Measure of the amount of work a team completes during a sprint, often used to estimate future capacity.

WIP (Work in Progress) Limits: Work-in-progress limits define the maximum number of tasks or stories a team or fractal can work on simultaneously. This helps maintain focus, reduce multitasking, and improve flow.

Frequently Asked Questions

(FAQ)

1. What is the F.I.T. Formula, and how does it work?

The **F.I.T. Formula** is a framework for creating high-performing Scrum teams. It has four components:

- **Dynamic Fractals:** Small, dynamic teams (three to four members) within the Scrum team that focus on delivering one story at a time, ensuring accountability and ownership.
- **WIP Limits:** Restricting work in progress to one story per fractal to improve flow and reduce multitasking.
- **Teaming:** Techniques like Mobbing, Swarming, and Pairing to promote real-time collaboration, resolve blockers, and enhance team cohesion.
- **Commitment Language:** Explicit, measurable micro-commitments made during Daily Scrums to promote accountability and progress.

These components work together to eliminate inefficiencies, foster collaboration, and build trust within the team.

---

2. How are Dynamic Fractals implemented in a team?

Dynamic Fractals are implemented by dividing your team into smaller, cross-functional sub-teams of three to four members. Assign each fractal one story at a time, ensuring no handoffs. Keep these Dynamic Fractals fixed during initial sprints (Shu stage) to establish clear ownership and minimize distractions. Fractal membership becomes self-organizing at the start of each sprint once the team stabilizes and matures.

---

3. What is the correct number of Dynamic Fractals for a Scrum Team?

Finding the correct number begins with determining the total number of engineers in the Scrum team, including developers and testers. Take the total number of engineers and divide by three. If there is a remainder of one or two, then create one or two Dynamic Fractals of four. If there are only five engineers on the team, then a pair will be necessary. See the table below. The Scrum Master and Product Owner are not members of a fractal.

Total Engineers	Two-Person Pair	Three-Person Fractal	Four-Person Fractal
3	0	1	0
4	0	0	1
5	1	1	0
6	0	2	0
7	0	1	1
8	0	0	2
9	0	3	0
10	0	2	1
11	0	1	2
12	0	4	0

After review of the table, one may question that if there are twelve engineers on a team, why not make two Scrum teams of six engineers? Frankly, that is preferable. However, there may be organizations, mostly due to economic reasons, that resist such a change, and the team is forced to remain on the larger size with twelve engineers.

---

4. How do Daily Scrums change in the F.I.T. Formula?

There are two fundamental changes to the Daily Scrum under the F.I.T. Formula:

- First, Commitment Language replaces the typical vague language often heard. The usual, three-question format is modified. See template.
- Second, once Dynamic Fractals, WIP Limits, and Teaming are in place, commitments are made at the fractal level on behalf everyone in the fractal. Fractal commitments are presented and reviewed in the Daily Scrum, and thus, there is no longer a need for individual commitments to be presented.
  - To aid in sharing fractal commitments, it is recommended that fractals do a brief sync to align on achievements and commitments before the Daily Scrum.
  - Teams may find that shifting to fractal commitments reduces the time required for a Daily Scrum. For example, instead of nine engineers providing updates, only three fractals are sharing their achievements and commitments.

---

5. How does sprint planning change in the F.I.T. Formula?

The F.I.T. Formula changes the approach and logistics of the Sprint Planning session in two fundamental ways:

- First, teams must be empowered to self-select their fractal membership. Fractal membership may change from sprint to sprint based upon sprint goals, technical interests, cross-training needs, desires to work with others, and work demands. This creates the Dynamic Fractals. Remember that fractal self-selection should follow the basic fractal guidelines.

- Second, Dynamic Fractals must be empowered to self-select their stories from the sprint backlog. This can be done during sprint planning whereby the team self-organizes to load-balance all committed stories across the fractals based upon logical story groupings, available skillsets, maintaining momentum around a collection of stories, and any other factors to create equitable and reasonable allocations. Alternatively, a Scrum team could establish a pull system for the Sprint Backlog so that when a fractal finishes a story, they pull the next highest priority.

- The most common method is where a Product Owner coordinates with the Scrum Master before sprint planning to understand capacity for the upcoming sprint. The Product Owner then slices stories from the product backlog that aligns to the team's available sprint capacity and presents them to the Scrum team. Once the Scrum team commits to the proposed stories, Dynamic Fractals are formed and then the fractals load-balance the committed stories. This method offers several distinct advantages over a pull system:

  - Clearer responsibility boundaries are established for all stories in the sprint backlog because Dynamic Fractals know the exact stories they must complete.

  - Increased ownership is established because Dynamic Fractals commit to all their respective stories at the beginning of the sprint.

  - More equitable load-balancing assignments are produced due to the collective wisdom and discussion while grouping stories.

  - Better opportunity for the fractal to plan their entire sprint because of the clearer responsibility. Dynamic Fractals can

218

then set intermediate milestones within the sprint for delivery. E.g., story #101 by day two of the sprint, story #102 by day five, and story #103 by day eight. This method helps guard against Parkinson's Law.

---

6. How does sprint review change in the F.I.T. Formula?

The F.I.T. Formula introduces no significant format changes to the sprint review. Teams may choose to showcase working software by fractals.

---

7. How does sprint retrospective change in the F.I.T. Formula?

The F.I.T. Formula introduces no significant format changes to the sprint retrospective.

---

8. How do I get team buy-in for using Dynamic Fractals?

Start by showing, not telling. Run a simulation where one group uses traditional methods, and another uses Dynamic Fractals to complete the same task. Most teams will see the benefits—faster delivery, clearer ownership, and less confusion—and willingly adopt the approach. Empower the team to experiment and adapt the fractals dynamically to suit their needs.

---

9. What if team friction worsens due to Dynamic Fractals?

If Dynamic Fractals create friction, address conflicts openly. Use Pairing or Mobbing sessions to rebuild trust and collaboration. Ensure roles and responsibilities within Dynamic Fractals are clear to minimize tension.

---

10. What do I do if team members resist Commitment Language?

Resistance often comes from fear of failure or perceived microman-agement. Emphasize that:

- Commitments are made by the person or the fractal, not imposed by any leader.
- Micro-commitments focus on manageable tasks that can be reasonably achieved by the person making the commitment, which makes success more likely.
- Unmet commitments are not punished; they are opportunities for transparent communication and learning.
- Commitment Language builds trust and helps the team collaborate more effectively.

Start small, encouraging people to make one clear commitment each day and gradually expand.

---

11. What if team members resist WIP Limits?

This is a common concern when starting with WIP Limits. Remind the team that:

- Limiting work in progress improves flow and reduces cognitive overload. Use examples or metrics to show how WIP Limits enhance delivery speed. Start with a manageable limit and adjust based on team feedback and velocity.
- Initial "slowness" is often the result of adjusting to a new rhythm. Once the team gets into the flow, progress accelerates.
- Remind the team that the WIP Limit of one in the F.I.T. Formula applies to stories. Dynamic Fractals may choose to swarm a story, whereby multiple tasks in progress are acceptable. Multiple people working on multiple tasks to deliver one

story is the definition of Swarming. Dynamic Fractals should set the WIP Limit on tasks to equal the number of people in the fractal.

---

12. What happens when a fractal gets stuck?

If a fractal is stuck:

1. **Call for help immediately within the fractal.** Mobbing allows the whole fractal to focus on resolving the blocker quickly.
2. **Escalate the issue during the Daily Scrum** to ensure visibility and alignment on next steps.
3. **Leverage the expertise of other Dynamic Fractals.** Collaboration across fractals can provide fresh perspectives. Call for a whole-team, cross-fractal Mobbing session.

The key is not to let a blocker linger. The F.I.T. Formula is designed to resolve issues in real-time.

---

13. Can Dynamic Fractals become too rigid?

Yes, fractals can lose their dynamic nature if not reviewed regularly. Dynamic Fractals are not intended to remain fixed. To keep them flexible:

- It is usually easier to implement fractals and hold them constant for the first few sprints. After this initial break-in period, fractals should become dynamic.
- Allow team members to reorganize fractals each sprint to cater to technical interests, to promote cross-training, to create opportunities to work with others on the team, or as the work demands change.
- Encourage open dialogue about how fractals are structured and empower the team to adjust within the F.I.T. Formula guidelines.

- Use retrospectives to evaluate whether the current fractal setup is effective.

---

14. How does the F.I.T. Formula reduce fear of conflict?

Fear of conflict is addressed through multiple components:

- **Commitment Language:** Structured discussions during Daily Scrums bring incremental progress and potential disagreements to the surface early, allowing for constructive debates before work progresses too far.
- **Teaming:** Collaborative techniques like Mobbing, Swarming, and Pairing create a culture of open problem-solving, where differing viewpoints are valued and encouraged.
- **Dynamic Fractals:** Small, trusted teams provide a safe space for members to express concerns or challenge ideas without fear of judgment.

Together, these practices create a more psychologically safe environment where constructive conflict becomes a catalyst for innovation rather than a source of avoidance.

---

15. What's the best way to introduce psychological safety?

Lead by example. Create an environment where team members feel safe to voice concerns, admit mistakes, and share ideas without fear of judgment. Regularly check in during retrospectives and actively address any signs of blame or fear.

---

16. How does the F.I.T. Formula help reduce social loafing?

The formula addresses social loafing by:

- **Dynamic Fractals:** Small teams increase accountability because each member's contributions are visible and impactful.
- **Commitment Language:** Daily commitments create transparency and a sense of responsibility to peers. People that do not commit or regularly miss commitments are highlighted.
- **Teaming:** Collaborative techniques like Mobbing, Swarming, and Pairing ensure everyone is actively engaged.

These practices make it difficult for individuals to disengage without affecting the team's progress.

---

17. How does Teaming differ from individual contributions?

Teaming emphasizes collaboration over isolation. Techniques like Pairing, Swarming, and Mobbing ensure team members work together on tasks in real-time, pooling knowledge and reducing delays caused by blockers or miscommunication. This collective approach drives faster and higher-quality results.

---

18. How does Teaming impact trust within the team?

Teaming techniques build trust by promoting equal participation and social sensitivity. Real-time collaboration strengthens relationships and fosters a shared sense of purpose.

---

19. What if our team struggles to adjust to Mobbing?

Mobbing can feel unnatural at first. Encourage the team to:

- Start with small, low-risk problems to build confidence.
- Set clear expectations that asking for help is encouraged, safe, and celebrated.

223

- Use retrospectives to address concerns and refine the Mobbing process.

Over time, as trust and collaboration grow, Mobbing will become second nature.

---

20. What if our team is already high-performing? Do we still need the F.I.T. Formula?

Even high-performing teams can plateau or face unforeseen challenges. The F.I.T. Formula provides a structured approach to sustain and scale performance:

- It builds resilience by fostering shared ownership and trust.
- It enhances adaptability through Dynamic Fractals.
- It provides a consistent way to address blockers and refine workflows.

The formula isn't just about fixing problems; it's about raising the bar and maintaining excellence.

---

21. How do we adapt the F.I.T. Formula for remote or hybrid teams?

The F.I.T. Formula works well for remote and hybrid setups with a few adjustments:

- **Dynamic Fractals:** Use digital collaboration tools (e.g., Zoom, Microsoft Teams) to keep Dynamic Fractals connected.
- **WIP Limits:** Visualize work using online Kanban boards (e.g., Trello, Jira, Azure Boards, Mural, Miro).
- **Teaming:** Schedule regular sync points and use virtual Mobbing, Swarming, or Pairing sessions to collaborate in real-time or address blockers.
- **Commitment Language:** Leverage digital collaboration tools (e.g., Zoom, Microsoft Teams) and/or digital platforms (e.g.,

Trello, Jira, Azure Boards, Mural, Miro) for recording commitments during Daily Scrums.

Psychological safety and clear communication are especially important in remote settings.

---

22. How can we measure the impact of implementing the F.I.T. Formula?

Track metrics like velocity, cycle time, and story completion rates. Monitor team engagement and qualitative feedback through retrospectives. Improvements in ownership, focus, collaboration, and accountability are key indicators of success.

Impact can be measured in several ways:

- Quantitative Metrics
  - Velocity (points completed per sprint).
  - Count (stories completed per sprint to measure throughput).
  - Cycle time (time taken to complete a story from start to finish).
  - Reduction in blockers or time spent stuck.
- Qualitative Metrics
  - Improved team morale and engagement (assessed through retrospectives and surveys).
  - Stronger alignment and collaboration within Dynamic Fractals (assessed through retrospectives and surveys).
  - Visible progress on the board, with fewer lingering tasks (assessed through observation).
  - An increase in Daily Scrum task specificity and accountability (assessed through listening and observation).
  - Social norm evolution around the F.I.T. Formula such as self-regulation of Commitment Language, micro-commitments, WIP Limits, engagement, etc. (assessed through listening and observation).

23. What's the first step to implementing the F.I.T. Formula?

Start with a single sprint experiment:

1. Introduce and practice Commitment Language during Daily Scrums.
2. Divide the team into Dynamic Fractals or determine if there are three people willing to try. If there are enough people willing to experiment, a team can start with a single, trial fractal.
3. Set a WIP Limit of one story at a time for each fractal in the trial.
4. Introduce and practice Teaming, even if it is with one trial fractal.
5. Use retrospectives to review the results and refine the approach.

Success breeds buy-in, so focus on achieving quick wins to demonstrate the value of the formula.

24. Why start with Commitment Language?

Commitment Language can be overlaid on existing practices and establishes trust and accountability quickly. It's a foundational practice that creates momentum for adopting other components of the F.I.T. Formula.

25. How do Shu, Ha, and Ri apply to implementing the F.I.T. Formula?

Teams begin in the Shu stage, following prescribed practices for consistency and stability. As they gain confidence, they enter Ha, experimenting with adaptations. In Ri, teams innovate, customizing practices to their unique context while maintaining core principles.

26. How does the F.I.T. Formula promote cross-functional skill development?

By working in Dynamic Fractals, team members often engage in tasks outside their typical expertise. For example:

- Developers might pair with testers to understand quality assurance better.
- Senior developers and junior developers may work together in the same fractal.
- Designers might join swarms to see how their designs are implemented. This natural cross-training strengthens the team's versatility and resilience.

27. How can we scale the F.I.T. Formula across multiple teams?

Begin by piloting with one team and gathering feedback. Use lessons learned to create a guidebook or training sessions for other teams. Ensure leadership support and ongoing coaching to sustain adoption.

28. Can the F.I.T. Formula work in non-Agile environments?

Absolutely. While initially designed for Scrum teams, the principles of Dynamic Fractals, WIP Limits, Teaming, and Commitment Language can apply to any team that values collaboration and efficiency. Tailor the practices to fit the specific needs and workflows of your environment.

Acknowledgements

Creating *Get Scrum F.I.T.—Fractals, Focus, and Flow for High-Performance* was not a solo effort. This book reflects the wisdom, support, and inspiration of many individuals who have shaped my understanding of teamwork, leadership, and Agile practices.

First, I want to thank the incredible Scrum teams and organizations I've worked with over the years, particularly those who allowed me to experiment, fail, and grow alongside them. Your courage and willingness to embrace change have been my greatest inspiration.

A heartfelt thank you to my mentors, colleagues, and peers in the Agile and Scrum communities. Your research, writing, and shared experiences provided a rich foundation for this book. Special acknowledgment goes to the authors whose works are cited throughout these pages—your insights are the backbone of many of the ideas presented here.

I also want to acknowledge the innovative use of generative AI in shaping the creative portions of the book's storyline. The narrative elements, including the challenges and growth of Team Swaggernauts to demonstrate Agile principles in action, were crafted with the help of this technology. This blend of human insight and AI creativity underscores how tools can enhance storytelling and problem-solving.

Finally, to you, the reader: Thank you for taking this journey with me. Whether you're a Scrum Master, Agile Coach, or a curious learner, I hope this book provides value, sparks ideas, and helps your teams thrive.

Let's keep raising the bar—together.

Final Thoughts

Throughout this book, we've explored how teams can transcend transactional changes and embrace transformational practices that foster ownership, alignment, and excellence. The Swaggernauts Guidebook isn't just a method; it's a mindset. It's a call to continuously evolve, challenge norms, and create systems that empower people to work together at their best.

As you take what you've learned and apply it to your teams, remember: transformation takes time, but the rewards are worth it. Every small win, every commitment kept, and every blocker resolved strengthens not just your team but the people within it.

The journey doesn't end here. Keep experimenting, keep learning, and keep raising the bar. Together, we can redefine what it means to work—and win—together.

Thank you for joining me on this journey.

Let's get Scrum F.I.T.!

About the Author

Dr. Anthony W. Montgomery is a transformational leadership expert, executive coach, and enterprise Agile strategist with over 20 years of experience developing leaders, teams, and systems that thrive under pressure. He is the creator of the F.I.T. Formula—Dynamic Fractals, WIP Limits, Teaming, and Commitment Language—a framework for revitalizing Scrum teams and fostering high performance through systemic change. Anthony holds a doctorate in Interdisciplinary Leadership and an MBA and is a certified coach. His career spans roles as a military officer, technology executive, and enterprise coach across industries including finance, healthcare, technology, and music.

www.ingramcontent.com/pod-product-compliance
Lightning Source LLC
Chambersburg PA
CBHW040918210326
41597CB00030B/5112